Guided Meditations For Overthinking, Anxiety, Depression& Mindfulness: Beginners Scripts For Deep Sleep, Insomnia, Self-Healing, Relaxation, Overthinking, Chakra Healing& Awakening

By Meditation Made Effortless

All Rights Reserved. No part of this publication may be reproduced in any form or by any means, including scanning, photocopying, or otherwise without prior written permission of the copyright holder. Copyright © 2020

Thank You!

Thank you for downloading this audio book. Today, we are in a crisis of mental health. The goal of this audio book is to help you adopt a meditation practice for life through calming meditation scripts that will keep you excited about and committed to the meditative lifestyle.

Once again, we thank you for downloading this audio book. It is a step in the right direction you have taken for a healthier, calmer, and happier you. We are sure you will enjoy the process!

Thank you!

Table of Contents

Introduction 1

Chapter 1 – Guided Meditation for Anxiety Relief (1 hour) 3

Chapter 2 – Guided Meditation for Stress Relief (30 minutes) 20

Chapter 3 Guided Meditation for Self Love (1 hour).... 29

Chapter 4: Guided Meditation for Developing a Wealth Mindset (1 hour) 43

Chapter 5 – Guided Meditation for Healing the Body and Becoming Healthier (1 hour) 56

Chapter 6 Guided Meditation to Balance the 7 Chakras (1 hour) 71

Chapter 7 Guided Transcendental Meditation (30 minutes) 83

Chapter 8 Guided Meditation to Overcome Addictions (1 hour) 90

Guided Meditation for Sleep and Insomnia Relief (1 hour) 103

Chapter 10 Guided Meditation for Releasing Anger (1 Hour) 118

Chapter 11 – Guided Meditation to get Over a Breakup (1 hour) 132

Introduction

Meditation is the must-have tool in this stressful and confusing time. There are many advantages of meditation practice. It can help control anxiety, manage panic attacks, reduce stress, improve relationships, reduce chronic ailments, control pain, get rid of fears and phobias, identify problem-causes and deal with them better, develop rapport with anyone in a group or individually, gain confidence, improve self-esteem, manifest desires, become more intuitive, and start to enjoy things one has hated or disliked in the past.

The meditation scripts in this audio book are designed with the modern lifestyle in mind. They are designed to help people having chronic stress-related disorders, anxiety and panic attacks, relationship problems, finances or job-related issues, anger-related problems, etc. There are scripts included to help balance and realign the chakras, get rid of addictions, sleep better, and even increase feelings of self-love and self-affection.

These are powerful scripts. They will take you through deep relaxation sequences and then re-wire your brain's programming and old, negative patterns imprinted on the subconscious mind. With regular practice, you can break past habits, overcoming repetitive problems, improve finances, sleep better, reduce chronic ailments, and improve relationships.

It is recommended that you use headphones or earphones while doing these meditations. Naturally, one must never listen to them while driving or operating machinery.

The benefits of mindfulness and meditation are well-documented today. We are simply presenting this ancient practice by customizing it for the modern user. If you are thinking about trying meditation, this is the audio book for you! Remember, success in meditation depends on your will power, your determination, and your desire to use these tools seriously and regularly.

Namaste!

Chapter 1 – Guided Meditation for Anxiety Relief (1 hour)

Hello and welcome to this guided mediation.

Before we begin, we will do a bit of warm-up exercise. Nothing too strenuous, just to get the body warm and the blood flowing. You see, a bit of physical activity before meditation is always a good thing because it helps in a deeper meditation.

So stand up and shake your hands and roll your shoulders a bit. Roll your wrists in clockwise and then in anticlockwise direction. You can jog in place of you feel like it. You can also roll your neck, counter-clockwise and clockwise for three to four rounds either way. Make sure you breathe easily and deeply during the warm up. You can also rotate your waist in clockwise and anticlockwise direction. Rotate your ankles similarly. Give a final shake to your wrists and palms. Dance or jog for a bit-anything to get the blood flowing a bit.

Okay, now you can relax. Make sure that you are in a comfortable place. It is recommended that you use headphones to listen to this guided meditation.

Please make sure you won't be disturbed for at least an hour during this meditation. Note that there is a possibility that you will relax and fall asleep or go into a deep trance. However, you are free to wake up and become alert immediately, should any situation so demand.

So this guided meditation is aimed at helping you overcome anxiety, and panic attacks. It can also help you overcome sleep-related issues and enable you to gently drift off into a quiet and peaceful slumber. Worry not – the meditation is still very powerful as your subconscious mind is still very much aware of my voice. So, you will still be able to reap its benefits –especially when you are faced with an anxiety-causing situation.

As you listen to this meditation frequently, you will eventually train your subconscious mind to reprogram its past conditioning, heal deep trauma, and overcome anxiety and panic attacks even when you are in the midst of one. All you need to do is to listen this meditation for at least a period of 21 days.

You can do this meditation any time of the day – morning, noon, or night. However, it is best not to meditate right after a large meal as that would cause you to go to sleep. It will help if you can do this meditation first thing upon waking up or right before you go to sleep. You can also listen to this meditation before your evening meal (right after work) so you can unwind and relax and get over the stress of the busy day.

Find a quiet and relaxed place to sit or lie down. You can use a couple of pillows behind the small of your back to support your spine. If you lay down, you can place a soft pillow under your neck to support the back. Just make sure that your spine is aligned and straight and your body is relaxed and loose.

If you choose to sit up and meditate, then I invite you to keep a yoga mat or sit by a comfortable bed so you can lie down and relax at the end – we will be doing some soothing and calming Yog Nidra or guided sleep meditation at the end of this session.

Make sure you are not too warm or cold and that you are dressed comfortably for these sessions. You can cover yourself with a light shawl or a sheet. It helps if you can light some incense sticks or candles to help you set a relaxation mood – but this is completely optional.

As always, do not listen to this meditation while driving or operating machinery.

Let us begin…..

Place your arms gently by your sides. You can keep your palms facing upward, open to the sky or you could keep them flat on your thighs if you are sitting up.

You can gently close your eyes if that is comfortable, although you can also leave them open. It is entirely up to you.

We will begin with some pranayams or deep breathing exercises. These will help your mind come to the present moment. Remember that your breath is the link between your mind and your body. Every time your mind starts thinking anxious thoughts; simply become aware of your breath. This will help you reduce that anxiety to a great extent and anchor your mind to the infinite present moment.

So, for the first breath, we will breathe in deeply to a count of 3..Go ahead breathe in deeply, fill those lungs completely with air....1 2 3....

Hold the breath to a count of 5.

And breathe out fully expelling all the air along with everything and anything that no longer serves you.

Take another deep breath in....this time up to a count of 5

1 2 3 4 5

Hold the breath to a count of 7

And breathe out, expelling all of the stale, unwanted air from those lungs.

I want you to relax more and more and sink deeper and deeper into a totally relaxed state.

Become aware of your thoughts. Accept your thoughts as they are. No matter what thoughts arise, good or bad, let them be. Just accept them and gently bring the mind back to the breath.

Become aware of your feelings – good feelings or bad feelings, just let them be.

Become aware of your emotions, good emotions, sad emotions, let them be..

Take a deep breath in and breathe out.

Become aware of your body weight – whatever it is 60 kilos, 120 pounds, just let it be. Place the entire weight on the seat or surface you are sitting on/or lying down on. Let the ground or chair or bed completely support you.

Become aware of your consciousness. Imagine your consciousness as a sphere around your body. In reality your consciousness is a lot wider and larger. Just become aware of this consciousness.

Now imagine a beautiful, healing white light entering your consciousness from the sky.

Let this healing light enter your body through the crown of your head.

Let the light circulate through the brain and the back of your head. You find your scalp and head relaxing deeply as this healing white light circulates throughout head area. Welcome any tingling sensations that may arise in this region. Just observe and let go-do not try to stop it.

The light now moves down through your forehead. If you want, you can slightly tense up the forehead and frown a bit. Then relax completely as the white light soothes every nerve and muscle in your forehead.

The soothing healing, creative light energy is now moving down throughout your face. It is relaxing your eyes and your eye muscles. It is soothing the nerves around and behind the eyelids. If you want you can squeeze your eyes momentarily and then relax them fully. The eyes are the windows to our souls. They undergo so much stress throughout the day. Closing your eyes from time to time heals and rests the strained nerves and muscles.

As the light enters your cheeks, you feel more and more relaxed. You feel your cheeks become more and more relaxed. The healing light energy is now gently soothing your nose, your mouth, your tongue, your lips and your jaws. You relax deeply as the light heals every pore, every cell, every muscle, making it loose, light, cleansed, calm, soothed, relaxed and filled with loving peaceful energy.

You are becoming more and more relaxed as the healing light moves down your neck inside your throat and into your shoulders. Relax those shoulders as the light relieves the aches and pains you have accumulated due to all that stress and anxiety.

Let the healing loving Universal light energy bring much needed relief in those tired and achy muscles. You can, if you want, hunch those shoulders and rotate the shoulder blades and the neck muscles a bit. Only if you want – otherwise just let it be. And relax as you listen to my voice.

Now the healing loving white light is traveling down your left arm into the left forearm all the way down to the fingertips. Each cell, muscle, and fiber in this area relaxes as the light soothes, heals, and nourishes it with unconditional love.

As the light travels down the right upper arm, forearm, and right fingertips, you become more and more relaxed. Your body becomes lighter and lighter. You just hear my voice...you hear nothing but my voice and you are totally relaxed..totally relaxed.

The healing light is now entering your upper back. It is soothing and relaxing those tired, achy back muscles and removing all of the accumulated stress, anxiety, and tension from these areas. If you want you can squeeze your back muscles and tense them momentarily before completely resting into a deeply relaxed state.

The white light is now traveling down your chest, into your heart center. It relaxes your heart muscles and fills your heart with unconditional love for yourself and for all your loved ones.

The light slowly moves down into your abdomen. It relaxes your stomach muscles and heals, calms, soothes, and rejuvenates the abdominal area completely. You are totally relaxed, totally relaxed. Your body is very light and a feeling of deep rest and relaxation is entering your body.

The light is now cleansing your lower body. It is entering into your pelvic area, down your hips, into your buttocks. Each and every cell in this region is becoming calm, relaxed, and completely healed with this cleansing loving light energy.

The beautiful white light is now traveling down the upper part of your legs. It is entering your left thigh, caressing your left knee, and going down your left calf, left ankle, down into the left heel and out the left toe. Every part of your left leg is becoming cleansed, healed, relaxed, and nourished with loving, soothing energy.

The peaceful white light is now entering the right hip, down into the right thigh, caressing the right knee, down the right calf, sliding into the right ankle as it relaxes every nerve, every cell. It fills your right foot, covering the right heel and out the right toe.

Your body is totally relaxed, totally relaxed – you are in complete harmony with the law of the Universe: the same laws that govern our subconscious mind, guiding us, healing us, and protecting us. Take a deep breath in and slowly exhale.

We will now say some affirmations. These affirmations will help you overcome anxiety and guide you in all those situations which trigger panic attacks. These affirmations begin with the powerful words I Am. I am – as Dr. Wayne Dyer says – are the two most powerful words in the Universe. They are the name of God – the Higher Power – the Universal energy – whatever you believe in.

Whatever you say after these words, you make them your reality. So, always use the words I Am with great care. Always use only positive sentences after these powerful words as they are the name of the Divine.

These I am and other positive affirmations for anxiety will help you reprogram your subconscious mind. You need not do anything – simply relax – and your subconscious mind will be listening to my voice. Let us begin

I am safe

I am totally calm

I am always protected by my guardian angels

I am in harmony with the Universe

I am deeply loved

I am healthy

I am beautiful

I am strong

I am always receiving the help I need

I am healing

I am peace

I am love

I am joy

I am always positive

I am brave

I am equipped to take care of myself

I am truly deeply and unconditionally in love with myself

I am aware that everything is happening for my highest good even though it may not seem that way at the moment

I am love

I am surrendering my troubles completely to the divine

I am being taken care of

I am healing from past trauma and looking forward to a vibrant and positive future

I am vibrant and energetic

I am totally alive and filled with unconditional love

I am amazing

I am awesome

I am energetic

I am fit and healthy

I am filled with self love and self respect

I am able to peacefully walk away from situations that no longer serve me

I am trustworthy and trusting

I am surrounded by those who have my highest good at heart

I am letting go of pain and suffering

I am wise

I am free and all is well in my world

I am in good company – I am never alone

I am completely in control of my thoughts and my actions

I am able to live in the present moment

I am able to breathe in peace and joy and breathe out stress and fear

I am always choosing love and happiness over anger, hatred, and fear

I am worthy

I am abundant

I am only focused on the good things around me

I am only filling my mind with positive thoughts

I am calm and peaceful in any given situation

I am completely relaxed in any given situation

I am able to quickly breathe out stress and breathe in strength and positivity

I am strong enough to handle anything that comes my way

I am able to let go of fearful thoughts and quickly replace them with positive and calming thoughts

I am completely in control of the situation

I am totally relaxed

I am always grateful for all the good things in my life

I am always safe and guided by my higher self

I am completely supported by the Universe

I am free and I am always able to choose freedom

I am completely and lovingly supported by this very supportive Universe

I am able to release and let go everything that no longer serves me

I am social and make friends easily

I am well liked by my friends, colleagues, and those around me

I am kind and generous to those in need

I am helpful and in return I always receive all the help when I need it

I am free of anxiety and will continue to remain so

I am slowly and steadily working towards my goals and my dreams

I am highly motivated

I am dedicatedly working towards my goals

I enjoy what I do and I work with passion

I am always receiving money and fortune abundantly

I am safe calm happy and totally in control

All is well in my world

Life is wonderful and everything is always working out for my highest good

Take a deep breath in and slowly breathe out...

Your sub conscious mind will remember these affirmations when faced with stressful situations.

I now invite you to lie down on your back if you are sitting up. We will do a relaxing Yog Nidra or a guided sleep meditation.

Relax comfortably on a bed or a yoga mat with your spine parallel to the ground. Keep your eyes closed. Make sure that your spine is straight, and your arms are loose by your side. Take a deep breath in and breathe out.

Take your attention to your left foot. Wriggle your left toe and then completely relax the left foot. Take a deep breath in and slowly breathe out. Relax and let go all your responsibilities. It is time to deeply relax and take this time for your mental and physical health and well being.

Wriggle your right foot and take your attention completely to the right foot. Moving upwards, bring your attention to the legs. Scan both the legs with compassion. Relax them. Your legs calves, ankles and feet are now completely relaxed.

Draw your attention to your pelvis. Squeeze the pelvic muscles ..hold tighter and tighter and relax them completely. Let go of all the stress and tension and simply relax. Now focus your attention on your abdominal region. Pull your navel back towards the spine – hold – hold – hold and then let go. Take a deep breath in a let go. Relax the stomach and abdominal region completely. Your stomach is now fully relaxed. You are feeling so calm, peaceful, and relaxed.

Take the attention to the chest and heart center. Breathe in deeply and fill the lungs with air. Let your chest expand for a moment or two before expelling all of the air out. Relax the chest muscles completely.

Shift your attention to your right shoulder and right arm. Tense the arm completely from the hands all the way to the shoulders. Tighter and tighter. Feel the muscles and ligaments in the arm tighten as they tense up completely. Feel the power in the right arm – before relaxing the entire right hand. You are deeply, totally relaxed.

Shift your attention to the left arm and left shoulder. Tense the entire left arm and hand as you feel the energy and power in it. Relax and completely remove the tension from this area. Feel your arm completely supported by the surface you are sleeping on. You are so relaxed.

Your fingers are relaxed, your wrist is relaxed and both the left and right arm, shoulder and hands are totally relaxed.

Now focus your attention on your face. Squeeze your eyes while keeping them closed. Relax those eye muscles. Tighten your jaw and feel it relaxed. Roll your tongue and then relax it completely. You can feel complete relaxation in your face, jaws, lips, eyes, cheeks, nose, and forehead. You are totally relaxed and peaceful.\

Now scan the entire body from feet to the crown of your head. Feel every cell, every nerve, every muscle let loose as you go deeper and deeper into a relaxed state. Each time you inhale and exhale challenge yourself to relax even more and more. Go deeper, sink deeper, get deeper into the deepest relaxation you have known.

Stay just as you are. Feel the peace, feel the relaxation and breathe it into every cell of your being. You are feeling so serene, so calm, so peaceful. Notice how your body is feeling right now. Memorize this feeling. Let it sink into every fiber of your being. Know that you can recreate this deep deep deep relaxation anytime you want.

You can continue relaxing or return t o the present moment by slowly becoming aware of your surroundings. Feel the surface beneath you. Picture the walls, the room, the ceiling, and your surroundings.

I am going to count from 5 to 1. With each number you will become more and more aware of your body and surroundings.

5..4..3..2...1

Slowly open your eyes. You are totally relaxed, refreshed, rejuvenated, and ready to take on the world. Have a great day ahead!

Chapter 2 – Guided Meditation for Stress Relief (30 minutes)

Welcome to this guided meditation for relieving stress.

We are living in a stressful time. Everything has changed and there is upheaval in the world. Someone may be suffering from stress related to job or finances; others may be stressed due to relationship issues. Students may have stress related to their workload and their future. In short: life is indeed stressful for most people today.

Things don't have to be that way. With a regular meditation practice, you can change your thoughts and your subconscious programming. Meditation can empower you to change your attitude and thoughts towards your stressful situation.

In this guided meditation, I will take you through a deep relaxation and guided imagery. You can perform this meditation first thing in the morning or right before drifting to sleep. You can even meditate anytime you are overwhelmed with stressful thoughts.

Before we begin, I would like you to get up and jog in place; just to get the blood flowing. You can even march in your place. You can do some body rotations as well – rotating the neck, the wrists, the shoulders and the feet in clockwise and counterclockwise directions. A low-intensity workout is always great to get your mind away from your stress-causing situation, get those endorphins flowing, and releasing negative emotions.

Okay, relax.

So let us begin.

Sit comfortably and easily and close your eyes. You can even choose to lie down comfortably on the bed or a yoga mat. Place your arms by your side with your palms facing upwards. Alternatively, if you are sitting up, place them open on your knees or in your lap.

We will begin by taking a deep breath in. Fill your lungs completely with the air, hold for a moment, and slowly breathe out.

One more time…breathe in, and slowly breathe out.

Take another breath in and slowly breathe out.

You are not asleep but you have taken the first step towards eliminating stress and complete relaxation. You can choose to use this practice to feel rested and even for drifting into a deep and relaxing sleep at the end of a stressful day.

Become aware of the sounds and noises in the environment. You just need to accept these noises and sounds in order to come into the present moment. In the past, these sounds may be cues that trigger stress and irritation, but now, you will use them to shift your perception and your awareness to any experience.

Inside your mind there is a deep place of relaxation, a *sea of tranquility*. You may not be aware of this place until this moment. But you can actually choose to access this place anytime you so desire. Now that you are aware of this place inside your mind, you only need to become aware of it each and every time you experience a stressful situation.

You can use this part of your mind to create, drift, dream, and float. For example, when you are stressed you can visualize the blue sky, an empty beach, warm sunshine, and the tranquil ocean. You look up to the sky and see a soft, fluffy cloud drifting slowly. You observe the cloud, its fluffy edge, and you feel it's pure energy and radiance.

As you watch the cloud becoming smaller and smaller as it moves towards the horizon, you become aware of your mind's ability to create its own experiences. The troubles and stressful situations now seem like a thing of the past. At this point, you are only aware of one thing: how deeply relaxed you are feeling.

If it is possible, I invite you to go even deeper into a relaxed state of mind and body. With every breath and exhalation, go deeper into a deep, deep, deep state of utmost peace, relaxation, and serenity.

Perfect. Now you are totally and utterly relaxed and you have a renewed sense of security and safety. You feel an overwhelming sense of a Higher Power taking care of all those situations that are causing stress in your life.

I will now give you some suggestions. You can choose to listen to those suggestions or simply drift off into a deep, peaceful rest. You need not do anything – just listen to my voice. Your subconscious mind will easily be able to internalize those suggestions now and at any time you wish to relax or have a peaceful and tranquil rest.

I recommend that you listen to this audio every night. With each session, you will find it easier to relax no matter where you are. You can immediately quiet down those nagging stressful thoughts and visit that special place deep inside your mind where there is peace and deep relaxation. This is also the place where creativity begins. Once you visit this place, you can immediately overcome the thoughts that are hindering with your sleep and your peace.

I invite you to deepen the relaxation. Loosen up those tense muscles and let go off any stressful thoughts. You know that you can open your eyes at any point should any situation demand so. But at this point, you are feeling so good, so totally relaxed that you can take this moment to simply relax and let go. For now, just let go of all responsibilities and deepen the relaxed state.

When you wake up from this deep, relaxing trance, you will feel so refreshed and peaceful, no matter what the day brings. You will feel complete rejuvenated and refreshed after this deep relaxation session. But right now, you must take this time to let go and deepen the relaxation even more. Right now, it is your right to go inward to that special place in the mind, and continue drifting in peacefully and happily.

I will now count backwards from 10 down to 1. With each number, enjoy the feeling and sensation in your body as you continue to drift deeper, and deeper, and deeper, into the deepest state of relaxation. Look for any sensation of coolness or warmth and use that as an anchor to let go of any lingering stress and drift deeper and deeper.

Ten, rest…nine, rest deeper, 8, you are totally relaxed, 7, 6,5, sink deeper, drift deeper, fall deeper, sleep. 4, not knowing where sleep begins, 3, total comfort 2 deepen the sleep,1 sleep…totally relax.

We will now do some affirmations to reprogram the mind to overcome stress right away:

I am strong

I am beautiful

I am loved

I am happy

I am peaceful

I am joyful

I am totally relaxed

I am letting go of tension and stress

I am totally in control of any given situation

I am letting go of fears and worries

My mind and body are calm and peaceful

I am positive and optimistic all the time

I am in control of my stress levels

I use relaxation techniques everyday to overcome and handle stress

I let go of all potential stress

I live a stress-free life

I live with work-life balance

I enjoy what I do

Money flows into my life

Everywhere I look, I see abundance

I find it very easy to overcome stress and tension

My mind is always calm and relaxed

I am always clear and focused

I work steadily towards my goals

Everything always works out for my highest good

I am always taken care of by a Higher Power

I live a healthy, calm, and relaxed life

I am calm and totally relaxed no matter what situation arises

My muscles are relaxed and loose

My body is full of energy and pain free

I accept situations easily and think with a clear mindset

I always think about the greater good and a positive outcome for all involved

I am always at the right time and at the right place

I am a winner

I am generous with my wealth

I am completely deserving of health, wealth, and abundance and I welcome these with gratitude

Every day in every way I al feeling better and better

I am becoming more beautiful and luminous every day

I breathe in relaxation and peace and breathe out stress and tension

I surrender to the Higher Power

My body is a miracle and I take care of it

I take good care of myself and I love myself unconditionally

I am proud of myself and all that I have achieved

I meditate easily every day without resistance

I choose love in every situation

As we near the end of this session, you can choose one of these affirmations and say it each time you start feeling overwhelmed with stress. You can simply say 'I am stress free' or choose a single word such as 'happiness' 'peace' or 'calm'. Every time you begin feeling stressed or anxious simply find that special sea of tranquility deep within you. Use your affirmation sentence or word and slip deeper and deeper into the deepest state of relaxation. This is the state of relaxation, peace, and calmness which you can find it anywhere you want- at home, work, or in any difficult situation.

You can easily bring yourself back to calmness and serenity and allow any temporary stress to pass without escalating. You can now choose to open your eyes or keep them close for a moment or two. Take some time to feel the floor below you and the air around you. Feel a renewed sense of energy in your muscles – allow yourself to feel this vitality coursing through the muscles of your body and your spirit. You are feeling refreshed, energized, and ready to be positive in any situation.

Chapter 3 Guided Meditation for Self Love (1 hour)

Welcome to the land of love! Self-love! That is what today's meditation is about!

Self love is often misunderstood and people confuse it or mistaken it with narcissism and selfishness.

In reality: self-love is the highest form of love. It is love akin to the love of guru/teacher or God; after all; the self, the Guru, and God are one and the same.

Many people do not love themselves enough and, resultantly, they seek substances or other forms of gratification. They chase love, thinking that another can make them happy. In reality; only you can make yourself happy. Happiness is always within us and not outside. If you believe that a person, thing, or experience will make you happy, then you are very much mistaken.

In this meditation, we will be going on a journey of self love. It will help reprogram your subconscious mind to respect yourself so deeply that every relationship you 'seek' will also deeply respect you. Everyone who comes in contact with you will show you the same unconditional love and respect that you show yourself and that you so fully deserve.

This is an hour-long meditation. So make sure you have that much time for yourself. You must take this time out daily for yourself so that you can fill your cup with unconditional love that you can share with the world. And believe me: the world needs love right now! It is best to do this meditation early in the morning before you begin your day. However, you may also do it in the evening after work, or before your evening meal.

Before we begin, I would like you to get up and jog in place; just to get your blood warmed up. You can choose to march in your place or simply perform a few body rotations– rotating the neck, the wrists, the shoulders and the feet in clockwise and counterclockwise directions. A low-intensity workout is always great to get your mind focused and get those endorphins flowing; releasing negative emotions.

So let us get comfortable.

Choose a quiet place where you will not be disturbed. Make sure that your gadgets and devices are all off. It is vital that you disconnect with the material world from time to time and go inwards to connect with yourself and with the Higher Power. You can light some candles and diffuse some essential oils – whatever gets you in the mood.

So let us sit comfortably. You can also do this meditation while lying down. And worry not: even if you drift off into a restful sleep, it is okay. Your subconscious mind will still be listening to my voice and that is all that you need to do.

Keep your palms in your lap or loosely by your side if you are lying down. You may also sit in a chair or on a bed or on the floor on a yoga mat. You can place a pillow beneath your hips or behind your back-whatever it is that is most comfortable for you. There are no hard and fast rules here. After all this is the meditation for self love and self care; so take care of your comfort – I know you will know exactly what you need for making yourself comfortable!

Let us gently close those eyes.

We will begin by taking a few slow, deep, deep, deep breaths.

Breathe in deeply…and slowly let it all out.

One more time, breathe in slowly and deeply through the nose…and exhale out slowly also through the nose.

And a final time, let us breathe in completely and fully…and slowly, slowly exhale out the unwanted air.

We will chant OM three times. Please note that OM is not a religious word here. It is the primordial sound that was heard when this universe came into existence. Science has now shown that there are many such primordial sounds and OM, AMEN, and AMEEN – which all sound so similar to each other-are nothing but the sounds that were heard at the beginning of creation. And they have been adapted by different religions as their own – when in reality, they were the First Sounds.

So taking a deep breath in say OM…………………………..mmmmm

One more time………..OM……………………………………

Om……………….

Feel the vibrations of the OM in your body.

I want you to take your attention to the top of your head. You may experience a bit of tingling, some sensations, or nothing at all. And that is okay. Just take your attention to the crown of your head. If there is a sensation, simply become aware of it. Do not judge, do not think this is good or bad. It just is and you just accept it.

Slowly draw the attention to the backside of your head. You might feel a need to scratch there, some itchy sensation or simply a tingling or even nothing at all. Just let it be. Take a deep breath in, and slowly breathe out.

Take your attention to the forehead. May be you can feel a sensation there: some kind of pressure or just the blood circulating or even some throbbing. As before, just let it be and move down to the eyes.

Relax those eye muscles. It feels so good to close those eyes. Take a deep breath in and breathe out relaxing the nerves, the muscles, and every fiber and cell behind those eyes. Go deeper and deeper into relaxed state as you slowly drift down to your cheeks and cheekbones. Relax the cheeks and every muscle in the face. Relax your tongue-let it simply settle down heavily into the lower jaw. Relax those jaw muscles. Take a deep cleansing breath in ...and slowly, very very slowly let it all out.

I want you to take your attention to your neck and throat area. Relax every muscle in the neck as you sink deeper and deeper into a relaxed state of trance. You might have some throbbing or pulsing sensation in the neck and throat area. Just let them be as you drift deeper, sink deeper, into a deepest state of relaxation.

Now you move your attention to the right shoulder and right arm. Do you feel a heaviness in those areas? Perhaps there is some throbbing or tingling there? Just let them be as you traverse the entire right arm, right shoulder, right hand, right wrist, right palm, all the way to the fingertips. Just observe and accept any sensation in these areas and you simply go deeper and deeper into a relaxed state.

Now move your attention to the left side. Observe internally what is happening in the left shoulder, left arm,, left forearm, left wrist, left fingers. Just relax and observe any sensation in these areas. Take a deep cleansing breath and slowly breathe out. Sink deeper and drift deeper into the deep sea of relaxation.

Now bring your attention to your upper back. Relax those upper back muscles and especially relax the spine. The spine is the seat of awareness as it has all the energy centers located upon it. It is a good idea to observe your posture throughout your day and ensure keeping your spine relaxed and straight. Breathe deeply into the upper back and relieve any source of tension there is. Observe the upper back and accept any sensation of stiffness, tension, or pain there may be. Breathe into those areas and become aware of the pain or stiffness melting away as you slowly breathe out.

Take your attention to your lower back. Relax the muscles of those lower back and breathe into any stiffness or pain there may be. Let those sensations go away with your exhalation. Sink deeper and deeper into relaxation.

Take your attention to the chest. Explore the chest muscles internally as your observe any feelings, sensations, even emotions arise. At this stage you are very relaxed and you might even feel sleepy which is completely okay. Simply breathe into the chest area and relax those muscles. Fill your heart center with unconditional love for yourself. Simply breathe in the loving energy from the benevolent Universe and store all that energy into the heart center. Breathe out the feelings of hatred, anger, judgment and criticism you feel towards yourself.

You can feel a vibration or pulsing in the heart area. Just linger here for a moment or two before moving down to the abdomen. Breathe in deeply to relax the abdominal muscles and slowly breathe out as your let go of pain, anger, and all that no longer serves you.

Relax deeper and deeper as you move your attention to the pelvic area. Relax the pelvic muscles and your hips. Breathe in deep relaxation to this area as you send loving, healing energy to your root chakra located at the base of the spine. Simply breathe out now to let go of any feelings of self-depreciation, anger, even hatred. Fill up the cup of love till it overflows with unconditional love from the Universe.

Take your attention to the right thigh and breathe in deeply to send loving kind energy to the thigh muscles. Accept any sensation of heaviness that may be present and slowly breathe out any remnant stress, tension, even pain. Let the right thigh become heavier and heavier; it is lovingly supported by the surface underneath you. Place the entire thigh on that surface. Know you are always taken care of by Shakti – the Universal Energy.

With that loving kindness, take your attention down to the right leg, right knee, right calf, right ankle, and the entire right foot from the heel to toes. You might experience some numbness or tingling in these areas. Accept them as they are. Breathe in loving energy to these areas and breathe out stress, pain, tension, and all that no longer serves you.

Take your attention to the left thigh and breathe in deeply to send loving kind energy to the thigh muscles. Accept any sensation of heaviness that may be present and slowly breathe out any remnant stress, tension, even pain. Let the left thigh become heavier and heavier; know that it is lovingly supported by the surface beneath you. Place the entire thigh on that surface. Know you are always taken care of by Shakti – the Universal Energy.

With that loving kindness, take your attention down to the left leg, left knee, left calf, left ankle, and the entire left foot from the heel to toes. You might experience some numbness or tingling in these areas. Accept them as they are. Breathe in loving kind energy to these areas and breathe out stress, pain, tension, and all that no longer serves you.

Now your body is so relaxed, so relaxed. You just hear my voice as you sink further into this loving energy that is circulating your entire body. You are now filled with unconditional love from Shakti – the Universal Energy of Divine love.

I want you to now think of a person who has been a teacher or a mentor, or even someone on a global level who inspires you as s/he has given so much to the world. Allow yourself to feel compassion and love towards that person. It could even be a historical person who has loved and given so much to the world like Mother Teresa or Gandhi. Right now, as you breathe in and out, I want you to feel unconditional love towards this person. It is easy since they have given so much to the world.

On the next breath in, I want you to think of a person who is close to you. It could be a close friend, a parent, a child, a boss, or even a lover. Someone that has touched you deeply and personally on some level. As you breathe in and out, feel loving kindness and gratitude for this person. In your mind, send that love and kindness towards that person. You might even smile a little as you think of this person with so much love.

Now, as you breathe in and out, think of a person you probably never think about when it comes to love. Yourself. When was the last time you felt kind, loving thoughts towards your self? When did you do something special or nice for yourself? Taking a spa is one thing; but really loving, caring for yourself on the deepest level is not top priority for most people. So, think about yourself as you breathe in and out and direct all of the loving, kind energy from Shakti – the Divine Source of Unconditional Love to yourself. You might even tear up a bit-become emotional or feeling like crying. And that is okay. Take your time to release these emotions as you send healing, loving and unconditional love to that Inner Child within you.

Appreciate yourself for being you. You are an important part of this Universe – you are God's Highest Creation and you must take the time to appreciate this beautiful creature that is You.

Realize that you deserve the best and that is what the Universe will give you. You have to believe it, say it, affirm it, and mean it. I am enough and I am powerful. We will now say some affirmations for Self Love. You can simply listen to them or repeat them silently in your mind or even out loud. Take a deep breath in and breathe out…

I am beautiful

I am lovable

I am love

I am filled with unconditional love for myself

I am awesome

I am amazing

I am aware, focused, and clear

I am brave

I am balanced

I am creative

I am completely at ease

I am clever

I am courageous

I am dazzling

I am energetic

I am enough

I am friendly

I am filled with unconditional love for myself

I am my favorite person in this world

I am good

I am grateful

I am healthy and make healthy choices

I am intelligent

I am joyful

I am kind

I am loving

I am magnetic

I am magnificent

I am naturally calm and balanced

I am optimistic

I am positive

I am at peace

I am radiant

I am splendid

I am talented

I am unique

I am virtuous

I am worthy

Take a deep breath in and slowly breathe out.

We will now sip into a Yog Nidra or a relaxed deep sleep. This will help your subconscious mind to reinforce the affirmations above and further deepen the already relaxed state. If you are sitting up, it is a good idea to lie down on a bed or yoga mat – keeping your eyes closed, lie down comfortably. Keep your spine parallel to the floor.

Take a deep breath in and slowly let it out. Take the attention to your left foot. Wriggle the left foot, shake the toes and then relax the foot completely. Next, take your attention to the right foot. Wriggle it and relax it completely. Now, tense the muscles of the left calf and relax them completely. Next, tense the muscles of the right calf and relax them. Let both your legs now relax completely. They may feel heavier or you might have some tingling or numbness in them. Just accept it. Breathe into the painful area and breathe out the pain.

Now take your attention to the left thigh. Squeeze the thigh muscles and then relax them. Do the same thing on the right thigh. Squeeze and then loosen the thigh muscles. Breathe into the thigh area and let out any remaining stress from the same as you exhale slowly.

Now squeeze the buttocks and relax them. You can breathe into the hips and exhale out any pain or discomfort there may be. Just rest the pelvic area completely now.

Take a deep breath and relax the abdominal muscles. Breathe in and breathe out completely as you relax the stomach and all the surrounding organs. Move upwards to the chest and relax the chest muscles. Deep breath in and out as you let go of any tension, anger, stress, and other negative feelings from the heart center.

Move the attention upwards to the left shoulder. Squeeze or tense the muscles in the left shoulder and let go. Relax the left shoulder completely. Flex the muscles of the left arm, left forearm, and the entire left hand. Squeeze, squeeze, and tighten before slowly releasing and letting go.

Move the attention to the right shoulder. Squeeze or tense the muscles in the right shoulder and let go. Relax the right shoulder completely. Flex the muscles of the right arm, right forearm, and the entire right hand. Squeeze, squeeze, and tighten before slowly releasing and letting go. Both your arms are completely relaxed and fully supported by the bed or floor. You are totally relaxed.

Now focus on your face. Squeeze and tense the muscles of the face, close the eyes tightly, and smile widely or frown a bit before completely relaxing the facial muscles. Your face is so so so relaxed and this is reduce the wrinkles, and giving you a smoother younger skin.

You now take your attention to the head. Your neck and head are completely relaxed and supported by the surface you are lying on. You are fully fully relaxed. You can sleep for a bit or simply choose to end this meditation by slowly returning to awareness. Do listen to this meditation daily for 21 days-once a day-maybe twice. This is how you can become more loving towards yourself.

I will count from 5 to 1. You can become aware with each number and return fully to the room. 5..4..3..2…1 become aware of your body and surroundings and slowly, gradually, open your eyes.

You are love, You are Peace, You are Joy!

Chapter 4: Guided Meditation for Developing a Wealth Mindset (1 hour)

This meditation will guide you towards abundance, wealth, and the financial life you deserve. You can, you absolutely can have what you want. We are all abundant beings. We all deserve the life of happiness and good fortune. We only need to believe it.

This meditation will help you manifest wealth and riches by re-programming your subconscious mindset into the money-making mindset. It will help write over past-programming that 'I am not worthy' or 'I am not good enough' and change it into 'I am enough' and 'I am worthy' mindset.

We have divided this session into different parts. In the first part, we will lead you into a deep, deep relaxation. This will be followed by some deep breathing for a few minutes. Deep breathing will help deepen the relaxation.

We will then ask our Inner Guides to help show us our true purpose. This will be followed by a period of 'Allowing' where we let the Universal Energy flow through us and help us create an abundance or wealth mindset. We will then have some affirmations for wealth and abundance, and this will be followed by gratitude for all the abundance that already exists in our lives. We will end the session with Yog Nidra.

I recommend that you do this meditation first thing upon waking up or last thing before going to bed. Just make sure that you haven't eaten a big meal 1-2 hours prior if you plan to meditate at bedtime.

Before we begin, I would like you to get up and jog in place; just to get your blood warmed up. You can choose to march in your place or simply perform a few body rotations– rotating the neck, the wrists, the shoulders and the feet in clockwise and counterclockwise directions. A low-intensity workout is always great to get your mind clearer, and get those endorphins flowing; releasing negative emotions.

Okay-now that is done, we can start with our meditation.

Get comfortable. You can sit up straight or lie down while doing this meditation. When we do Yog Nidra at the end of the session, we will be lying down, so please keep a mat or make sure there is a comfortable bed nearby. This way; you can lie down during the Yog Nidra session.

If you are sitting up, simply keep your spine erect. If you are lying down, it is best to lie down upon your back and not sideways. You can keep a small pillow to support your back or neck, whatever is most comfortable.

Take a deep breath in and breathe out slowly.

We won't be closing our eyes just yet. Instead, I want you to focus on a spot directly in front of you, may be on a wall. Keep staring at the spot as your inhale and exhale slowly. Now, slide your sight to another spot directly below the first one-may be 6 inches below the first one. Look at this second spot for 5 to 10 seconds as you continue to inhale and exhale slowly.

I will count down from 10 to 1, keep your eyes open and keep looking at the second spot. 10…9…8…7…6…5…4…3..2…1

Inhale and exhale slowly once and slowly, very gradually close down your eyes to about 50% close. Breathe in and out. Close your eyes now to 75% close – your eyes are just open a small slit. Breathe in and out. Finally you may slowly close your eyes 100%.

Continue to inhale and exhale slowly. It is always a good idea to notice the breath when we get stressed about whatever situation one may be dealing with. The breath is the only constant in life. No matter where we go, the breath goes with us. You can cultivate awareness of the present moment simply by becoming aware of the breath – it is the anchor.

We are going to completely notice and study our breath for a few moments. How does the breath feel as it slowly enters the nose? What sensations do you observe when the air touches the tips of the nostrils? Is it cool or warm? Is there a tingling sensation as the breath enters the nose and gets filtered by the million tiny hairs inside the nose?

Observe and notice the breath rate. Is it slow or fast, is it deep or shallow? How many breaths are you taking in a minute? We never pause to think about the breath – when in reality, it is our constant companion. When we are angry, our breath becomes short and sharp. When we are happy, our breath is longer, more relaxed.

Just focus on the breath as you continue to simply inhale and exhale slowly and deeply. Which nostril is drawing in more air? How does the area above the upper lip feel as the breath touches it while exiting and entering?

Can you find the pause between each breath? That tiny pause is the present moment awareness. The *now* or the *present* moment is entirely focused between two breaths. As the breath exits and fades, observe the tiny pause at the end-just before the incoming breath starts again and rises and peaks…and at the peak, there is a tiny, tiny pause that gradually fades into the exhale – just like a wave. A wave has crests and troughs and between each crest and trough there is the pause – the pause that we can notice to bring the mind to present moment awareness.

Continue to take a moment to explore and study each breath..each inhale as it fades into an exhale and each exhale as it rises into an inhale. Breathe in –notice the pause…breathe out..notice the pause…

Now, pay attention to the abdomen. Observe the stomach as it rises as you breathe in and slowly falls as you breathe out. Take a moment to observe this rise and fall. Continue watching the abdominal area as your breath naturally enters and exits the body.

Now, I want you to fully expand your abdomen on the next incoming breath. Let the belly expand as much as possible and as you exhale, deliberately bring your navel towards your spine.

On the next inhale, again bloat the belly completely and on the next exhale, pull the navel back towards the spine.

Continue this deliberate breathing…expanding the tummy area on the incoming breath and pulling it backwards as you breathe out. Try to do it as effortlessly as possible-without any jerking movements, any noises, or too much effort. Try to relax as much as you can while continuing this deliberate breathing with expansion on the in-breath and contraction on the out breath. We will do this few more times…very gently, very slowly. Take all the time to really breathe into the tummy and expand it and slowly and gently let the air out as you pull the stomach backwards.

Now relax and breathe normally.. ..with very normal and natural inhalation, followed by normal, natural exhalation. The breath is our anchor. It is the present moment and it is our grounding mechanism to bring you in the 'now'.

Right now, as you pay attention to your breath, we will also pay attention to our wealth. We are surrounded by wealth and abundance. There is abundance of trees and the leaves, and the grass, and the animals. There is abundance in the form of a warm bed and hot water for showering. There is abundance in that morning cup of coffee and the fresh-smelling, clean sheets. Everywhere you look you will see abundance. You will cultivate this attitude of seeing abundance wherever you go.

When we focus on abundance instead of lack or poverty, the Universe gives us even more abundance. Even if your bank balance is not what you want it to be, notice the potential for wealth creation inside of you. Notice your ideas, notice your creativity, notice your ability to work hard or study hard.

Take a moment to think about your strengths. You may be trustworthy. You may be hardworking, You might have great memory, and you may be very intelligent, cheerful, thrifty, clean, brave, and good. All of this is abundance and when you focus on these qualities, you nurture them. Energy flows where attention goes. So it is good to focus on these things from time to time.

You may not own the fanciest wheels in town, but you have a car or dependable public transportation to get you by. You may not be eating in fancy restaurants night after night but you have warm meals to nourish you every day.

When you measure yourself with these standards, then you, my dear are rich compared to millions of people who sleep on empty stomachs. You are at least in the top half of the worlds wealthy. The question is: how do we move to the top 1%?

The key to more wealth creation is to be grateful for what we already have. That is the law of attraction. You have to feel happy right now. And always be grateful.

In this relaxed state of mind, we will now ask our Inner Guides to bring us the wealth we seek. Let us call upon the Divine, benevolent energy of the Universe to fill us with love, abundance, and gratitude.

Imagine there is a lavender color energy flowing from the sky into your being. It first touches the crown of your head and slowly circulates through your brain. This is the healing, loving energy from the Universe. It is a creative energy that will help you do more, be more, get more, seek more.

This beautiful lavender energy is now flowing through the front and back of your head. It touches your forehead and slowly soothes away any tension there is. It also circulates through your cheeks, mouth, nose, eyes, tongue, jaws, and lips. This is a healing, soothing energy that will help you relax and bring your body into complete state of relaxation.

The healing light is now moving through your neck and throat. It flows down your arms, through the shoulders all the way down to the fingertips.

The lavender energy is now circulating through your chest and upper back. As it moves through your body, your body becomes more and more relaxed. You mind becomes clear, cleansed, and totally relaxed.

The lavender energy is now moving through your abdomen. It circulates through the organs and flows into your hips and lower back. The creative energy is now flowing through the upper part of your legs, down through your knees, into the calves and ankles, all the way through the heels and toes of your feet.

Your entire body is now totally relaxed, totally relaxed. Your mind is clear, cleansed, and in perfect harmony with the law of vibration.

Now, whatever you see on the screen of your mind, you can manifest it in your material world. Your mind will take you to beautiful places and this can become your reality. Imagine that you are living where you really want to live. You are doing what you really want to do. The healing lavender energy along with the Law of attraction will bring you the life you seek and deserve.

Remember: what you seek is seeking you. Ask and ye shall receive.

I want you to imagine friendships so powerful so strong - you are surrounded by friends and loved ones. You feel a rush of love for all these important people in your life. You are living in a beautiful house surrounded by your loved ones.

You love what you do. You are the best at your work. You have a steady source of passive income and wealth just flows freely into your life.\You are able to go faster, do more, achieve more with minimum effort. You love what you do. Your passion flows into your work. Your colleagues love you and they look up to you. You inspire people to become like you-hardworking, happy, vibrant, alive, strong, passionate, and full of energy.\

You are able to achieve work-life balance with ease. You have plenty of time to pursue your hobbies. You have time and money to travel and see all those beautiful sights that the world has to offer.\

You are healthy and fit. You have the time to workout and get in the best shape of your life. Every cell of your body is vibrating with health and positive energy.

You can wake up early and meditate every day and find the time to invest in your health.. You can easily achieve your daily to-do lists. You can achieve more in a short span of time.. You hardly need to put in efforts as everything just gets done quickly and effortlessly. You find the right people to help you and you help them in return. You can go faster, stronger, you can do more achieve more because the creative energy of the Universe is flowing through every cell of your body.

And you are totally relaxed. Totally relaxed. You just hear my voice and you know that your Inner Guides along with the universal lavender energy is coursing through every cell of your body. You have the strength and the tools to do more, achieve more, get more, all in a calm and relaxed state of mind.

We will now do a few affirmations to reinforce the money-making mindset. You can also say these affirmations every night before bed. When you say these affirmations at night, you will reprogram your subconscious mind and overcome past conditioning that you are not worthy or that you aren't enough.\

I am wealthy

I am wise

I am hardworking

I am passionate about my work

I love what I do

Money flows into my life easily and freely

I am surrounded by my Inner Guides who help me when I need

I am grateful for all the abundance already surrounding me

I give freely and help others

I achieve my true potential and help others achieve their true potential.

I willingly give and graciously receive

I am kind

I am rich

I am surrounded with love, health, wealth, and happiness

I am worthy

I am deserving of all the abundance in my life

I am able to achieve work-life balance

I live where I really want to live

I love my job

I have a steady source of passive income

I am rich beyond my wildest dreams

I am healthy, wealthy, and wise

I get the help whenever I need it

I am in the right place at the right time

Everything always works out in my favor

If you are sitting up, please lie down on your back.

We will slip into a yog nidra- deep sleep for further relaxation.

As you lie down, take your attention to your feet. Wriggle your toes and relax them completely. Now slide the attention upwards to the calf muscles. Tense the calves of both the legs and relax them. Take your attention to the thighs. Contract the thigh muscles and relax them fully. Squeeze your buttocks and relax. Breathe in and breathe out and relax more and more. Slide the attention to the stomach. Breathe in and expand the stomach and slowly breathe out as you let the air out. Take the attention to the chest. Expand the chest area and relax fully. Squeeze the shoulders and relax them. Take the attention to the arms, squeeze all of the muscles and tense them and then relax both the arms fully. Take your attention to the face. Relax the facial muscles. Relax your head. Relax completely.

You are developing a strong desire to listen to this meditation from time to time. Every day for at least 21 days, you will listen to this meditation. You will go to a quiet place and totally relax within a millisecond. You will listen to this meditation once a day, may be twice for a period of at least one month. And see the abundance flow.

I will now count from 5 to 1. With deep gratitude, you will become aware of all the abundance in your life - with each number. We are going from 5 to 4 you are becoming aware of your surroundings, from 4 to 3 you are becoming aware of your body from 3 to 2 slowly turn to your right side, from 2 to 1. Slowly sit up and open your eyes. Om shanti Om!

Chapter 5 – Guided Meditation for Healing the Body and Becoming Healthier (1 hour)

Health is wealth. When health is lost, we become miserable and it can impact all other areas of our lives as well. When you practice meditation every day, your mind becomes healthier and no disease or illness can thrive in a body where the mind is healthy. So, meditation can bring overall wellness and health and improve all aspects of your life.

This guided meditation will help instill health and well-being in your entire body. With regular meditation practice, you can regenerate new, healthy cells and remove or flush out diseased cells. Meditation and mindfulness can help you stay in the present moment so you will feel joyful and happy all the time. And when there is joy and happiness, there is no room for sickness or ill-health.

As always, it is recommended that you do this meditation in the morning or listen to it while in bed, at night. Morning meditations are better since they set the tone for the day so you can actively and energetically take on the day and all that it brings with it.

Before we begin, I would like you to get up and jog in place; just to get your blood warmed up. You can choose to march in your place or simply perform a few body rotations– rotating the neck, the wrists, the shoulders and the feet in clockwise and counterclockwise directions. A low –to moderate-intensity workout is always great to get your mind clear and get those endorphins flowing; releasing negative emotions.

Okay-now that is done; we can start with our meditation.

Let us sit comfortably in a chair or on a floor. Please keep your neck and back straight and relaxed. Try not to keep your neck and shoulders stiff, just relaxed and loose. You can slowly close your eyes or simply keep them open if you want. No hard and fast rules here.

Concentrate on your breathing. Simply become aware of the incoming and outgoing breath. You don't have to try too hard – just do it as effortlessly as you can. Focus your attention on the feeling of air as it enters and exits your body. Do not try to control your breathing – don't try to make it fast or slow. Just let your natural rhythm take over. You simply be the observer. If your mind wanders, and it will, gently bring it back to the breath.

And your mind will wander. You might think of the tasks or to-do lists ahead or perhaps about your health. You might be distracted by pain or simply may be feeling depressed or even worried about the outcome of your health. Maybe you are awaiting some test results which might be making you anxious. You may not be sleeping as well as you'd like to and this insomnia may be adding to your woes and making matters worse.

But for the moment, I want you to forget all of that and just focus on your breath. The mind however, will keep wandering. You might feel like getting up and leaving this meditation. You will feel restless and impatient but it helps to gently set a resolve that you will stick along for this hour.

Gently bring the mind back again and again to the breath. Simply observe where the mind goes and bring it back. Use the breath as an anchor. Each time a thought or worry occurs, just acknowledge it. Do not analyze it or judge it. Just observe it and return to the breath.

Let go all thoughts of something special waiting to happen. You just focus on the next breath. Life is nothing but the stringing of one breath after the other. There is no truth but the breath.

The beauty of this practice is that you can do it anytime you feel anxiety or pain. You can do it in the shower, while you are eating, when you are running errands, etc. Simply bring back your attention to the breath. You don't need to find any special time to do this. You can just do it anytime. Significant research has been done on this practice and these studies all show that the practice of breath awareness and mindfulness can relieve stress, anxiety, ease pain, improve concentration, and even help in manifesting whatever you want. And that also includes manifesting good health. So bring back your attention again and again to the breath. Breathe in and out, deeply and fully. If your mind wanders, back you bring it to the breath!

Now, I want you to become aware of what is bothering you. Perhaps it is the fear of getting or being sick, or a nagging pain in some part of the body. It may be a chronic illness or an acute condition that has suddenly arrived.

Simply become aware of it. For example, if you have a migraine, become aware of the throbbing in the brain. Perhaps the pain is in the neck and temples or between the eyes. Maybe you have nausea and sensitivity to light and sounds. Just become aware of it. Accept the pain, be the pain.

Now I want you to repeat this phrase silently in your mind: *'alert mind, calm body'*. You can repeat it three times.

Alert mind, calm body

Alert mind calm body

Alert mind calm body.

Inhale slowly and deeply and imagine the breath coming into your body through the soles of your feet. Now exhale slowly and imagine the breath moving back down your legs and out of your feet. Allow your jaw, tongue, and shoulders to relax completely.

Now breathe in deeply and allow your belly to expand. Bring in fresh air to nourish your body. Breathing out simply bring your attention to the rhythm of your breathing. In and out...in and out, in and out. Do not try to control your breath in any way. Just let your breath come in naturally and exit naturally. Simply attend to the natural rhythm of your breath.

In your mind's eye, imagine yourself standing on a beautiful beach. The sky is a brilliant blue and there are fluffy clouds floating slowly by. Take in a moment to enjoy the scenic beauty. Drink in the colors. Breathe the fresh air in and exhale out completely. Repeat one more time. Inhale and exhale.

Now become aware of the beautiful beach around you.

Become aware of the warm beating down comfortably upon your body. There is a pleasant, warm salty breeze that brings in the scent of the ocean. You inhale this fresh scent and exhale it completely feeling relaxed and refreshed.

You become aware of your feet in the soft sand below leaving behind footprints as you slowly start to walk along. The waves are gently lapping at your feet.

The water's temperature is perfect-not too warm or cold. The waves gently lap at your feet forming little bubbles and cleaning your feet off the sand that accumulates between your toes. You continue walking leisurely along the shore feeling grateful to be here in this divinely beautiful place. The beautiful sky and the aquamarine ocean stretch endlessly and you are alone and yet you feel totally safe and relaxed.. You feel the delightful waves gently lapping at your legs. The sand is firm and soft and here and there you see beautiful sea shells glistening in the sand. The gentle breeze feels perfect on your face and neck.

In the distance, you hear seagulls calling out to one another and gently gliding across the sky. You are feeling so peaceful, so divinely peaceful. In the distance, you see a shack with an umbrella covering a cozy chair. You decide to rest a bit and walk over to the shack and relax on that chair. A feeling of deep peace settles over you.

You lie back on the ultra comfortable chair and close your eyes. You let your neck, shoulder and back relax into that soft and plush cushion of the chair. You are completely relaxed and you feel totally safe. You can feel the sun warming your body and the gentle breeze and the sound of the waves relaxes you further and further. The umbrella shields your eyes from the sun's rays and a feeling of total peace and relaxation wash over you. Somewhere you hear soothing music, far away in the background. The music deepens your relaxation.

Your body is totally relaxed and your mind is hearing the soothing notes of music that fall upon your ears. All the pain leaves your body and total relaxation, health and well-being seep into every cell of your body.

Deep relaxation enters your feet and toes and you drowsily notice them getting heavier and heavier. You completely relax your legs into the chair and the warm cleansing sunlight nourishes your legs filling them with total health and peaceful relaxation. Every cell in your legs experiences complete health and well-being.

The peaceful feeling travels up from your legs into your thighs and you relax both thighs muscles and knees completely. Health and well-being seep into every cell of your thighs and upper legs as your mind relaxes and body becomes calm and infused with healing light energy.

The cleansing healing energy now penetrates deep into your pelvis as you completely relax your groin muscles. This healing creative light energy infuses every cell of your groin muscles, cells, nerves, and tissues –filling them with warmth, love, health and well being. Deep deep relaxation is flowing throughout your pelvis as you totally relax and sink deeper into the deepest relaxaiton.

The healing, soothing energy now enters into your abdomen. It relaxes the muscles of your abdomen deeper and deeper. It infuses all your organs with healing light and rejuvenates all of the cells. Every cell in the abdomen is now radiating with total health and happiness. All the organs in the abdomen are now totally relaxed and infused with health and well being.

Deep relaxation now travels upwards into your chest right through your heart center. The healing light energy helps you relax every muscle and cell of your chest. Each cell now radiates with total health and well being. The healing, loving energy floods your entire chest to remove diseased cells and replaces them with healthy and vibrant rejuvenated new cells. The energy traverses and caresses the muscles of your entire back. All the stress, tension, and pain leave your back, neck, and spine. Every cell in the upper and lower back is now vibrating peacefully with health and joy.

You are totally relaxed and your mind is completely at ease, peaceful, and calm. The healing light energy now enters your shoulders and traverses down into your arms. Every cell of both the arms is completely at ease and radiating with health. The light infiltrates through every nerve, every muscle, and every tissue to cleanse, heal, relax, soothe, and infuse them with total health.

You are totally relaxed, your mind is at ease. You are calm and full of health.

The healing light energy now travels up your neck, through your throat. It heals all the nerves, cells, and tissues it touches. Every cell in the neck and throat is now relaxed and vibrating with good health.

The healing light energy now completely touches your facial muscles. It traverses your cheeks, your jaws, your tongue, mouth, eyes, nose, and lips. Every part is receiving this healing light energy. Your face is totally relaxed as the light soothes away lines, wrinkles, and other signs of aging. The healing light is now stimulating collagen and elastin giving you a mini face lift. Your face is becoming younger, smoother, healthier and full of radiant beauty and well-being.

Your eyes are totally relaxed, every nerve, every muscle is relaxed, your eyelids are filled with vibrant relaxing energy that heals and soothes away all of the pain and tiredness.

You now relax your forehead as the healing loving universal energy soothes away the frown lines from it. The light now covers your head and the back of your head. There is immense sense of relaxation and peace flowing throughout your brain and head.

Your entire body is now totally relaxed. The warm light has healed every cell and restored health and well being in your entire body. You are also in complete alignment with all the Universal Laws. You are in alignment with the Law of Vibration and the Law of Attraction which will help bring good health and all that you desire.

This is the perfect time to reinforce positivity and what better way to do that than through affirmations. Let us make these statements of good health so that your subconscious mind imprints these positive statements and help you manifest good health.

I am healthy

I am at peace

I am well nourished

I am loved and cared for

The Divine Universal energy is flowing through me

I am in perfect harmony with the Universe

Disease leaves my body and only good health flows through me

Every cell in my body is vibrating with good health, peace and joy

I am happy

I am joyful

I practice mindfulness with ease

I am brave

I am fearless

I know that everything happens for the best

The Universe is working for my greatest good

My mind is always calm no matter what the situation may be

I am relaxed

I sleep well

I eat nourishing foods and make healthy choices

I am motivated to workout

I am in the best shape of my life

I have great metabolism

I am able to drop the pounds with ease

I breathe deeply and fully with awareness

Good health flows through my entire body

My family is healthy and we are aligned in our health goals

I am surrounded by people who love me and motivate me

I make friends easily and we bring out the best in each other

I release all fear and replace it with love

I am filled with love health and kindness

I am accepting of any changes that occur in my life

I am supported in my efforts to care for myself

I practice loving kindness towards myself

I know that self-love is the highest form of love

I have all the courage and strength I need to look after myself

There is abundance of love, health, and peace in my life

I release all the root cause of my pain and ill-health

I am balanced in body, mind, spirit, and emotions

I help others make healthy choices

I inspire others and motivate them to follow a healthy lifestyle

I lead from a place of love and balance

I am full of strength, grace, wisdom, and peace

I believe in myself

I set goals and easily achieve them

I have the courage to fulfill my goals

My body, mind, and spirit are in perfect harmony with the Laws of the Universe

I know that the Divine cares for me

I am surrounded by guardian angels who watch out for me and keep me safe

I am protected

I am safe

I receive all the divine guidance I need to make the right choices

I am conscious of the endless possibilities around me

I am grateful for all the good things in my life.

I am beautiful

I am wise

I am conscious of the divine wisdom and beauty in me

I release my physical pain and my attachment to it

I am proud of the body I have and excited to shape it to be more of what I want

I am stronger than my cravings

I choose only positive thoughts

I am love

I am health

I am peace

I am joy

As you complete these affirmations, you experience a feeling of total bliss and joy. Peace and health wash over your body. You feel a Divine presence blessing you. You feel a rush of immense gratitude flowing through you. You feel grateful for your loved ones and send them a blessing. You feel refreshed, centered, balanced, and totally relaxed.

You feel vibrant, energetic, and alive and totally ready to take on the day and all that it brings with it. You feel blessed and you feel total harmony with the law of vibration. You feel grateful for the nourishing foods and the abundance of health, wealth, and happiness in your life.

You slowly get up from the chair and walk back towards the beach and the gentle sea. You dip your hands in the cool water and take a handful of water in your palms. You then release the water and with it, you let go of all the pain, sickness, negativity, and illness. The sea promptly washes it all away leaving you with peace, health, and unconditional love and joy.

As you complete your meditation, you feel totally ready to come back home. I will count down from 5 to 1. With each number, you will become more and more aware of your body and surroundings. Giving thanks for the vibrant health, you slowly come down from 5 to 4, to 3, to 2, to 1..open up your eyes, you are totally relaxed and healthy….. Have a wonderful day ahead.

Chapter 6 Guided Meditation to Balance the 7 Chakras (1 hour)

In this meditation, we will balance the 7 chakras or the energy centers located on the spine starting from its base all the way to the crown of the head. We won't go into too much detail about what chakras are. It is, however, a good idea to know that each chakra or energy center is linked to certain parts of the body as well as to our materialistic world, our thoughts, our states of consciousness, and even to all that happens or befalls us. For example, a misalignment in the heart chakra can cause an imbalance in relationships and could even affect finances. Likewise, an imbalance in the throat chakra can cause communication issues.

So let us correct these imbalances so that you can lead healthier, richer lives.

Before we begin, I would like you to get up and jog in place; just to get your blood warmed up. You can choose to march in your place or simply perform a few body rotations– rotating the neck, the wrists, the shoulders and the feet in clockwise and counterclockwise directions. A low-intensity workout is always great to get your mind clear and get those endorphins flowing; releasing negative emotions.

Okay-now that is done, we can start with our meditation.

We will begin with a deep relaxation technique followed by meditation for each chakra.

It is best to perform this meditation by sitting upright with the spine erect. You can place a pillow behind the small of your back and relax comfortably and easily either on the bed, floor, or a chair. Just keep the spine erect. Let your hands remain open in your lap, facing the sky . If you are sitting in a chair, you can sit with your feet firmly planted on the ground. If you are sitting on the bed or the floor, simply maintain the lotus position.

Let us begin. Close your eyes and take a deep breath in. Slowly breathe out.

Draw your attention to the right leg. Contract the muscles of the right leg and then slowly relax them. Your right leg is getting heavier so rest it entirely on the surface on which you are sitting. Breathe in deeply and breathe out fully. Relax.

Draw your attention to your left leg. Contract the muscles of the left leg and then slowly relax them. Your left leg is getting heavier, so rest it entirely on the surface on which you are sitting. Breathe in deeply and breathe out fully. Relax both the legs completely. Your feet are relaxed, your ankles are relaxed and loose.

Relax your calf muscles of both the legs. Relax your knees of the left and right legs fully.

Draw your attention to the right thigh. Tense the right thigh muscles and hold it for a couple of moments. Now let go and relax completely. Relax your right thigh and feel the energy flowing through it.

Draw your attention to the left thigh. Tense the left thigh muscles and hold them for a couple of moments. Now let go and relax the left thigh completely. You can feel the energy flowing through it. Notice both the thighs. They may feel warm, or you might experience some tingling, numbness, etc. Just let both the thighs sink deeper and deeper into the ground. Make a resolve to keep both the legs very still throughout the entire duration of this meditation.

Now draw your attention to your fanny. Tense the muscles of the fanny and hold them in. Hold tighter and tighter and now let go. Relax the pelvic muscles and feel the energy swirling in the area.

Next, bring your attention to the abdominal muscles. You can tense the abdominal muscles by pulling your navel backwards towards the spine. Hold for a moment or two and then relax completely bring the stomach back to normal and breathing with your natural rhythm. You are sinking deeper and deeper into relaxation. Your body is becoming lighter and lighter and you are feeling calm, peaceful, and totally relaxed.

Take in a nice deep breath, feeling your abdomen rise with the air and then let the air all out – you are feeling totally peaceful, relaxed, and content.

Shift your attention to your right arm. Tense the entire right arm from the hands to the shoulders holding still and feeling the energy and the power. Now let go and relax completely surrendering fully. Your right arm is completely relaxed from your shoulder all the way to the tips of your fingers. Let your arm be completely supported by your lap and let it get heavier and heavier as it relaxes more and more.

Draw your attention to your left arm. Tense the entire left arm from the hands to the shoulders holding still and feeling the energy and the power. Now let go and relax completely. Your left arm is completely relaxed from your shoulder all the way down to the tips of your fingers. Let your left arm be completely supported by your lap and feel it get heavier and heavier as it relaxes more and more.

Both your arms are totally relaxed. Your fingers are relaxed, your arms are relaxed, your shoulders are relaxed, your elbows are relaxed. Feeling comfortable and totally at ease, make a resolve to completely keep both the arms still throughout the duration of this meditation.

Bring your attention to your face. Squeeze your eyes and relax them completely. Feel the eyelids relax, the eye muscles relax, the lines are the eyes, the eyebrows, all relax. Relax your cheeks and jaw. Let your tongue relax and roll forwards in your mouth as it sinks down into the lower part of the mouth. Relax your lips. Relax your forehead. Relax your nose. Breathe in and out through the nose once and then relax completely. Your face is now so relaxed. Make a resolve to keep your face still throughout the duration of this mediation. Relax more and more and let go.

Now scan your head, the crown of the head, the back of the head and relax them fully. Relax the neck and back muscles make a resolve to keep the head, neck, and back completely still throughout this mediation. Breathe in and out and relax fully.

You can sink deeper into a deep state of relaxation by scanning the body inwardly. Scan it from the top of the head all the way down to the feet and out through the toes. Your feet are relaxed, your calves and knees are relaxed, your thighs and the back of the thighs are relaxed, your pelvic area is completely relaxed, your abdomen is relaxed, your chest and back are relaxed, your shoulders and neck are relaxed, your face and head are totally relaxed.

Feel yourself relax even more with each exhalation.

Now take your attention to the root chakra also called the Muladhara chakra. It is located at the base of the spine. Inhale deeply into the base chakra and exhale out completely. You can feel the energy tingling into the Root chakra. Imagine the Root chakra vibrating and rotating as beautiful red flower spinning around its axis. The powerful energy circulates throughout your perineum, the base of the spine, and the lower three vertebrae. Breathe into the root chakra as it balances and aligns itself correcting all imbalances. You can visualize your Root chakra growing tentacles that reach deep inside the core of the earth. You become one with the earth as your Root chakra draws energy from Mother Earth. All the resources you need are present here. The earth returns the love to your Root chakra through vibrations. Feel your root chakra vibrating with peace and love. Welcome this energy as it sends healing love and light to all your root organs, your legs, thighs, pelvis, and lower back. Now that your Root chakra is balanced, you begin to trust the Universe knowing that you will receive all the guidance, the grounding, and the healing you need from it. Your worries melt away with each breath as you deepen your connection to the Mother earth. Notice how your root chakra feels awake and alive vibrating with peaceful, loving energy.

Now take your attention to the Sacral chakra- also known as the Svadhistana chakra –located just a few inches above the Root or the Muladhara chakra. Inhale deeply into the Sacral chakra and exhale out completely. You can feel the energy tingling into the

Sacral chakra. Imagine the Sacral chakra vibrating as an orange colored flower spinning around its axis. The powerful energy circulates throughout sacral area including your sex organs. Breathe into the Sacral chakra as it balances and aligns itself correcting all imbalances. You can visualize your Sacral chakra getting its energy from water – its associated element. You become one with the water element as your Sacral chakra draws energy from it. All the resources you need are present right here. Waves upon waves of water returns the love to your Sacral chakra through gentle vibrations. Feel your Sacral chakra vibrating with peace and love. Welcome this energy as it sends healing love and light to all your Sacral organs, your spleen, reproductive organs, the pelvis, the lower back. Now that your Sacral chakra is balanced, you begin to trust the Universe knowing that you will also receive all the guidance, the grounding, and the healing you need from it. Your worries melt away with each breath as you deepen your connection to Water element. Notice how your Sacral chakra feels awake and alive vibrating with loving energy.

Now take your attention to the Solar plexus chakra- also known as the Manipura chakra –located just a few inches above the navel. Inhale deeply into the Solar plexus chakra and exhale out completely. You can feel the energy tingling into the Solar plexus chakra. Imagine the Solar plexus chakra vibrating as an yellow colored flower spinning around its axis. The powerful energy circulates throughout solar plexus including your abdominal organs. Breathe into the Solar plexus chakra as it balances and aligns itself correcting all imbalances. You can visualize your Solar plexus chakra getting its energy from Fire – its associated element. You become one with the warm fire element as your Solar plexus chakra draws energy from it. All the resources you need are present right here. Warmth radiates all through your Solar plexus chakra. Feel your Solar plexus chakra vibrating with peace and love. Welcome this energy as it sends healing love and light to all your abdominal organs, your stomach and intestines. Now that your Solar plexus chakra is balanced, you begin to trust the Universe knowing that you will also receive all the guidance, the grounding, and the healing you need from it. Your worries melt away with each breath as you deepen your connection to Fire element. Notice how your Solar plexus chakra feels awake and alive vibrating with loving energy.

Now take your attention to the Heart chakra- also known as the Anahata chakra –located right where your heart is. Inhale deeply into the Heart chakra and exhale completely. You can feel the energy tingling into the Heart chakra. Imagine the Heart chakra vibrating as an emerald green colored flower spinning around its axis. The powerful energy circulates throughout heart including your chest and lungs. Breathe into the Heart chakra as it balances and aligns itself correcting all imbalances. You can visualize your Heart chakra getting its energy from Air – its associated element. You become one with the Air element as your Heart chakra draws energy from it. All the resources you need are present right here. Loving energy radiates all through your Heart chakra. Feel your Heart chakra vibrating with peace and love. Welcome this energy as it sends healing love and light to all your heart and lungs. Now that your Heart chakra is balanced, you begin to trust the Universe knowing that you will also receive all the guidance, the grounding, and the healing you need from it. Your worries melt away with each breath as you deepen your connection to the Air element. Notice how your Heart chakra feels awake and alive vibrating with loving energy.

Now take your attention to the Throat chakra- also known as the Vishuddha chakra –located in the throat. Inhale deeply into the Throat chakra and exhale out completely. You can feel the energy tingling into the Throat chakra. Imagine the Throat chakra vibrating as blue colored flower spinning around its axis. The powerful energy circulates throughout throat including your neck, throat, the thyroid gland. Breathe into the Throat chakra as it balances and aligns itself correcting all imbalances. You can visualize your Throat chakra getting its energy from Ether – its associated element. You become one with the Ether as your Throat chakra draws energy from it. All the resources you need are present right here. Warmth radiates all through your Throat chakra. Feel your Throat chakra vibrating with peace and love. Welcome this energy as it sends healing love and light to your thyroid, throat, neck. Now that your Throat chakra is balanced, you begin to trust the Universe knowing that you will also receive all the guidance, the grounding, and the healing you need from it. Your worries melt away with each breath as you deepen your connection to Ether element. Notice how your Throat chakra feels awake and alive vibrating with loving energy.

Now take your attention to the Third Eye chakra- also known as the Ajna chakra –located in between the eyebrows on the forehead. Inhale deeply into the Third Eye chakra and exhale out completely. You can feel the energy tingling into the Third Eye chakra. Imagine the Third Eye chakra vibrating as deep indigo colored flower spinning around its axis. The powerful energy circulates throughout Third Eye including entire forehead, eyes, and eyebrows. Breathe into the Third Eye chakra as it balances and aligns itself correcting all imbalances. You can visualize your Third Eye chakra getting its energy from Light – its associated element. You become one with the pure white Light as your Third Eye chakra draws energy from it. All the resources you need are present right here. Warmth radiates all through your Third Eye chakra. Feel your Third Eye chakra vibrating with peace and love. Welcome this energy as it sends healing love and light to your eyes, eyebrows, and forehead. Now that your Third Eye chakra is balanced, you begin to trust the Universe knowing that you will also receive all the guidance, the grounding, and the healing you need from it. Your worries melt away with each breath as you deepen your connection to Light element. Notice how your Third Eye chakra feels awake and alive vibrating with loving energy.

Now take your attention to the Crown chakra- also known as the Sahasrara chakra –located on the crown of your head. Inhale deeply into the Crown chakra and exhale out completely. You can feel the energy tingling into the Crown chakra. Imagine the Crown chakra vibrating as a brilliant purple colored flower spinning around its axis. The powerful energy circulates throughout Crown including entire head, top and back of the head. Breathe into the Crown chakra as it balances and aligns itself correcting all imbalances. You can visualize your Crown chakra getting its energy from pure Spiritual Energy of the Universe . All the resources you need are present right here. Warmth radiates all through your Crown chakra. Feel your Crown chakra vibrating with peace and love. Welcome this energy as it sends healing love and light to your head. Now that your Crown chakra is balanced, you begin to trust the Universe knowing that you will also receive all the guidance, the grounding, and the healing you need from it. Your worries melt away with each breath as you deepen your connection to Universal Spiritual Energy. Notice how your Crown chakra feels awake and alive vibrating with loving energy.

All your chakras are now balanced and you are ready to come back to awareness. I will count from 5 to 1. With each number, you will feel more and more centered and more aware of your body and surroundings. 5, wriggle your toes, 4, move your shoulders, 3, and become aware of your surroundings, 2, become aware of your mind, 1 – eyes open.

It is recommended that you do this meditation at least once a day for 21 days to keep your chakras balanced and active. Namaste!

Chapter 7 Guided Transcendental Meditation (30 minutes)

Transcendental meditation is a mantra based meditation. It can quickly take you into the deepest state of consciousness. Usually, the meditation mantra is given by a guru or a master who is basically an awakened meditation teacher with decades of meditation practice. In this audio, we will use the word Om in place of the mantra. In reality, the personalized mantra is customized for every disciple and is typically a word which is very similar to Om, such as Shum, Rrrum, etc. But, for the purpose of this guided meditation, we will use Om.

Om is a primordial sound without any religious connotation attached to it. It is the sound that scientists have heard when they sent probes into space to find out what the Universe sounded like. It is believed that Om was one of the sounds heard during the creation of this planet and life.

You can do this meditation in the morning or evening. It is best not to do this meditation after having a big meal or when you are very sleepy. Remember, meditation is not sleeping. In meditation, you remain awake and aware but you are in a deep trance focused only on the present moment. It is only at this point that your brain goes into a theta state of deep relaxation.

Before we begin, I would like you to get up and jog in place; just to get your blood warmed up. You can choose to march in your place or simply perform a few body rotations– rotating the neck, the wrists, the shoulders and the feet in clockwise and counterclockwise directions. A low-intensity workout is always great to get your mind clear and get those endorphins flowing; releasing negative emotions.

Okay-now that is done; we can start with our meditation.

So let us get comfortable. Sit easily and comfortably and close your eyes. Resolve to sit still for the entire duration of this meditation.

We will begin by chanting Om three times.

Take a deep breath for the first Om….deep breath in Ommmmmmmmmmmmmmmm

Again breathe in…Ommmmmmmmmmm

Third time let us breathe in Ommmmmmm

Relax

Take your attention to the top of your head. Breathe into the top of your head and relax with a gentle, slow exhalation. You may notice some tingling, numbness, etc in the head or scalp. Let it be. Just observe it. Just observe the head internally. Explore the brain, the tissue, the nerves, the cells. Now explore the head externally: take a look with your mind at the scalp. Take a look with your mind at your hair. If there is any sensation on the scalp, just let it be.

Now move your attention down to the forehead. Explore the forehead internally and externally. Let any sensations that arise just be. There may be some tingling – just observe it. There's no need to react. Simply be the observer.

Let the attention slip down to the face. Explore the cheeks, scan the inside of the mouth. Relax the tongue, jaws, and teeth. Relax the eye muscles. Relax the eyelids completely. Breathe in slowly and fully and let it all go with a slow deliberate exhalation.

Move your attention to your throat and neck. Relax the throat and neck completely. If there is any sensation in the neck, just observe it. No need to do anything. Simply be.

Take your attention to the heart center. In your mind, observe the heart and think of the word or mantra Om. Anytime thoughts start coming into your mind, this is what you will do. You will simply take your awareness to the heart and in your mind, say the word Om. You will not say this sacred word aloud; -you will simply say this mantra Om in your mind. And every time you do so, you will sink deeper and deeper into relaxation.

Now scan your upper back and shoulders. Any sensation that you feel here, simply welcome it. There may be tension in your shoulders, perhaps even some pain. But you simply become the observer of this pain or sensations. Again, if any thoughts arise, take your attention to your heart center and mentally say the word Om and sink deeper into relaxation.

Now take your attention to the right arm. Scan the entire right arm from your shoulder to the tips of your fingers. Observe any itching or tingling you may feel here. Simply observe – do not judge or try to fight it. Simply scan the entire right arm from shoulder to the finger tips. And again, if any thought arises, simply take your attention to the heart center and think of Om. And immediately sink into a deep sense of blissful relaxation.

Now take your attention to your left arm. Scan the entire left arm from your shoulder to the tips of the fingers. Observe any itching or tingling you may feel here. Simply observe – do not judge or try to fight the sensation. Simply scan the entire left arm from shoulder to the finger tips. And again, if any thought arises, simply take your attention to the heart center and think of the precious and sacred mantra Om. And immediately find yourself sinking into a deep ocean of blissful relaxation.

Take your awareness to the abdomen. Scan the organs in the abdomen-the stomach, the intestines, the kidneys, etc. Scan the abdomen internally and externally. Feel your clothes' fabric touching your stomach. Be the observer and let whatever sensation is there simply be. If any thoughts or emotions arise, simply take your attention to your heart center and think of the precious and sacred mantra Om. And immediately find yourself sinking into a deep ocean of blissful relaxation.

Take a deep breath in and slowly let it out.

Take your awareness to the pelvic region. Simply explore the genitals and your sex organs internally and externally. Explore your buttocks. There may be some tension or tightness or pressure in your hips. Feel the pressure of the ground or surface you are sitting upon on your buttocks. Be the observer without any judgment. Accept the numbness or tingling or even pain that you may be experiencing in this region. And if any other thoughts arise, simply take your attention to the heart center and say Om in your mind. And immediately find yourself sinking into a deep ocean of blissful relaxation.

We will now scan our legs. First scan the right leg internally and externally from the thigh to the knee to the calf all the way down to your toes. Accept any sensations there may be like tingling, numbness, the feel of your clothing, may be even pain. Accept these sensations fully. Do not judge. If any thoughts arise, simply take your attention to the heart center and think of the precious and sacred mantra Om. And immediately find yourself sinking into a deep ocean of blissful relaxation.

Now, scan your left leg internally and externally. Traverse the leg from the left thigh, to the knee, to the calf, to the heels and toes. Accept any sensation there like tingling, numbness, pain, the feel of the fabric, or even pain or heaviness. Do not judge these feelings. Simply become aware of their existence. If any thoughts arise, simply take your attention to your heart center and think of the precious and sacred mantra Om. And immediately find yourself sinking into a deep ocean of blissful relaxation.

Your body is now totally relaxed. Your mind is calm. You are completely at ease. Sit in this blissful awareness for a few minutes. If any thoughts arise, simply take your attention to your heart center and think of the word Om. Do not say it aloud, simply feel the word Om and its vibrations as it draws you into total relaxation and peace.

(Give the listener some time to meditate on their own with the OM mantra).

Take a deep breath in and breathe out. I will count from 5 to 1, with each number, become more and more aware of your body and your surroundings…5, 4,3,2,1…slowly and gradually open your eyes. Om Shanti Om.

Do this meditation daily to experience its lasting benefits in all aspects of your life.

Chapter 8 Guided Meditation to Overcome Addictions (1 hour)

If you have come to this guided meditation, then it is a good sign of great things to come. Because it means that you know you have a problem and are willing to take measures to overcome it. The truth is that we are all addicted to something or the other. We all look for external or material things to give us joy. In reality; all of the joy we need is right within us. When we learn to truly love and accept ourselves for what we are, then we no longer need something or someone else to do that for us.

First of all, having an addiction does not mean that you are a bad person. However, it does mean that you are hurting yourself and therefore you must take the steps to stop.

Addiction can come in various forms. It can be an addiction to sex, drugs, alcohol, or smoking. It could also be an addiction to sugar, coffee, or gambling, In any case, all of these can be bad if one overindulges in them.

So let us meditate. It is best to do this meditation once a day for at least 21 days so it deeply engrained in your subconscious mind. Any good habit you wish to form can become deeply rooted in your brain in 21 days as this is the time period needed to change the brain's neural pathways. And that is why, we recommend 21 days of daily meditation.

Before we begin, I would like you to get up and jog in place; just to get your blood warmed up. You can choose to march in your place or simply perform a few body rotations– rotating the neck, the wrists, the shoulders and the feet in clockwise and counterclockwise directions. A low-intensity workout is always great to get your mind clearer and get those endorphins flowing; releasing negative emotions.

Okay-now that is done, we can start with our meditation.

Close your eyes, and start becoming aware of your breath. Let your breath come in and go out as naturally as possible. Do not try to change or control your breath. Let it be as natural as you can. Simply observe it.

Now, I want you to imagine a staircase. It is a safe, spiral staircase leading down to a beautiful garden. I want you to descend this staircase and, as you do, with each step, I want you to relax more and more. You take the first step and immediately sink deeper into relaxed state.

You take step 2, and deeper you go. You feel some of the tension releasing from your muscles and different parts of your body. As you sink deeper, you take step 3, and deeper you go.

Slowly the tension is leaving every muscle, every fiber of your being nd you sink deeper, go deeper, drift deeper.

Deeper deeper deeper into the deepest state of relaxation.

You take step 4 and 5 and go even deeper.

You take step 6 and sink deeper.

You take step 7 and 8 and I wonder if you can go even deeper.

You take step 9 and sink into a totally relaxed state.

And at the step 10 – you sink your feet into a soft, grassy soil. You notice the peace and contentment around you. The contentment fills you deeper and sweeps through your entire being.

You breathe in the fresh air and fill up your lungs with air. As you walk along a beautiful, safe garden path – you feel like you are leaving behind all the materialistic pleasures and objects behind you. You leave behind all those substances that no longer serve your body.

You proclaim in your mind – ' I release the need for all substances that no longer serve my body'.

You can feel your entire body fill with peace, contentment, and relaxation. You feel joy and bliss enter every cell of your being. Each and every cell and fiber of your being vibrates with health, joy, and total peace and relaxation.

You proclaim in your mind: 'I am free of unhealthy cravings. I only accept that which nourishes my body. I only seek healthy, sustaining substances.'

As you walk in the soft grass you feel the warm sunshine on your body. You feel the warmth spread through your face. Your throat, shoulders, neck, back, chest, arms and legs feel warm ad comfortable. You feel deep relaxation spreading throughout the body.

You smile at the flowers. The air has a sweet perfume of fresh flowers surrounding you. There are flowers in virtually every color, yellow, red, orange, and purple, pink, blue. You notice the gently perfumed breeze caressing your body. As the breeze washes over you, every cell vibrates with life. You feel totally calm, cleansed, healed, relaxed, and alive with joy.

As you walk along, you notice you are coming to a boardwalk leading to a cliff. You are totally drawn to this cliff which is safe and comfortable to walk up to. You continue to walk in the warm and pleasant environment with the breeze soothing you and the sunlight keeping you comfortably warm.

As you reach the cliff, you see the vast expanse of the serene blue ocean. The beautiful blue water is calming and relaxing and standing at the cliff's edge very safely, you see the water sparkling in the sun.

You breathe in deeply filling your lungs with the fresh air and exhale slowly. You feel so totally content and relaxed. You are so happy to be here and you are so happy to feel so alive and vibrant and healthy. Most importantly, you are so happy to be you.

You take a look at your life and you feel so content. You are surrounded by so much beauty, joy, and abundance. The Universe has always guided you and helped you. You feel grateful to be alive. Being alive is the greatest gift you have and the universe has bestowed it upon you.

So you take a moment to feel grateful and say 'thank you'.

You breathe in and out deeply and slowly and in the distant you hear seagulls. You can see the seagulls gliding across the water. The waves crash upon the shore and you feel totally alive.

You absorb the beautiful peace and serenity around you and feel so thankful –with complete gratitude, you proclaim- 'I am alive healthy and content. Every breath instills health in me. I choose health and stay away from all that no longer serves me'.

Opening your arms before the beautiful vista, you delight in realizing that you have left sorrow, illness, and pain behind you. Spreading your arms wide you look towards the sky and feel the sun spreading your chest with warmth.

You feel healthy, peaceful, and grateful to be alive. You feel free. Oxygen fills your lungs and as you inhale deeply and exhale slowly you feel vibrant and joyful and alive.

Every breath fills you with peace and life. You have never felt so alive before this.

You sit on a comfortable rock near you.

Images fill your mind. You see yourself indulging in your addiction. It may be viewing porn or smoking or drinking. You do not judge-simply observe. You only see the pain behind your actions. You understand that you are indulging in these behaviors because you are running away from something. Let those emotions arise. If tears come, do not try to stop them. Understand that self love is the highest form of love. Feel your heart center fill with unconditional and overwhelming love for yourself. You are your own lover and you take a vow never to indulge in destructive behaviors. You understand that you are enough and that you are always supported by the benevolent universe. Take a moment to process all these feelings and emotions.

You can now clearly see the reason behind these actions. You realize that you are a pure soul filled with nothing but a need for love. You are a soul that only wants unconditional love and you have to give that love to yourself. When you love and accept yourself fully, the Universe also fills you up with love.

We will now throw away all that has transpired in the past. So you pick up a stone lying at your feet and toss it over the cliff. The stone hits the water and sinks out of sight. With that symbolic gesture you release your past. You proclaim yourself to be rid of the past. You let go of guilt and anger. You replace those feelings with unconditional love for yourself. We now say some affirmations to reinforce this:

I am enough.

I love myself.

I release my past without judgment.

I let go of all substances and addictions that no longer serve me

I forgive myself of all my past mistakes – they are lessons that I will use to move ahead and better myself.

This is a new day. I go forward in peace.

I am free of any addictions and desire for substances that no longer serve me

All withdrawal effects and cravings are leaving my body.

My subconscious mind supports me and helps me overcome my cravings with ease.

My body balances withdrawal with ease.

I crave and enjoy only healthy foods.

I release my past and forgive myself. I move forward with love and peace.

My body, mind, and spirit are healing. Every day I am getting better and better.

My subconscious mind powerfully supports me. II am free of all desires for substances that do not serve my mind, body, or spirit.

My body balances withdrawal effects.

I am a non smoker.

With every breath, my lungs are becoming stronger, cleaner, healthier, and more alive.

I am totally in control of my behaviors and my life.

My subconscious mind is powerful and it supports me fully.

I am free of unhealthy desires and cravings.

I think and speak positive statements about myself

I enjoy enriching relationships and these are based on mutual respect.

I am in control of my actions and the words I speak.

I am content and happy with this blessed life.

I understand that it is a privilege to be alive and I am deeply grateful for life.

Each and every day, I am closer to my ideal weight

My health gets better and better each day

I only crave healthy foods that nourish my cells with life. Only healthy foods crave my attention, excite my taste buds, and satisfy me.

My body easily digests nourishing foods and is brimming with health, happiness, and joy.

Breathing in and out slowly and deeply, you become aware of the seagulls. Warm sunlight bathes your entire body with love and light. The entire universe seems to cheer you on. You call out to the Universe and say

I am free I am free. I am transformed.

Breathing in and out, the light and peace transform you. You feel like a changed person. Now that you are free, you can take on anything. You can quickly finish all your projects on time. You see yourself going faster, stronger, and doing better. You see yourself achieving more and more. You see your friends and family cheering you;. They are jumping up and down, clapping for you and screaming your name.

You are in perfect harmony with the law of vibration. You feel so alive, so aware of this wonderful world that you are a part of. You are so relaxed, so relaxed. You are living where you really want to live.. You are doing what you really want to do. In all aspects of your life – you are doing better, achieving more, you are inspiring people. Your colleagues look up to you. Your friends and loved ones admire and respect you. They want to know the secrets to your success. You help them as philanthropic thoughts move in your mind.

You want to graciously give and receive. You help others overcome their shortcomings and unhealthy cravings. You help them make healthy choices. You bring them on board of your health plans and they love you for helping them change.

You inspire others and teach them about self love. You are a beautiful human being and you are an important part of the Creation. You are God's highest creation.

You get up from the rock and start walking back. You become aware of how joyful, vibrant, and happy you are feeling. You notice how comfortable you feel with yourself, your body, and your thoughts. Feeling totally relaxed and blissful, you repeat over and over to yourself – I am so happy, I am so grateful, I al free.

You feel the warm glow of knowing that you are enough. You know you need nothing or no one to fulfill you. You say to yourself over and over that you are happy and grateful. You are likeable. You want to show these qualities to everyone. You suddenly wish your friends and loved ones were around and as if, by magic, you see a group of people in the distance.

As you approach the people, you see familiar faces. They are all smiling at you with pure love in their eyes. Your heart expands with warmth and love as you approach your loved ones. They gesture you to come over and you move towards them with a spring in your step as you wish to show them the new YOU. You keep remembering all the while that you are likeable, loveable, and enough.

You approach the happy group and they take turns hugging you. You proclaim- I enjoy happy, enriching, and mutually fulfilling relationships. I am free of competing. I strive for the greater good fo the community. I want everyone to feel abundant as they have come in contact with me. ' Smiling with outstretched hands your head held high, you feel proud of yourself and all that you have achieved till now. You feel lighter and lighter, more and more joyful, happier and happier. You feel stronger and stronger by the minute. You support yourself with kind words and you speak kind words to all around you.

As you sit with these loving souls, you feel stronger and stronger by the minute. You feel more vibrant and alive. You say – " I control the words I speak; I am filled with vitality\.

As you leave the group, everyone joins in clapping for you and touching your back to pat you. They are so proud of you for taking control of your life.

You happily walk back through the garden. You walk towards the stairs and pass the sweet-smelling flowers. You are pleasantly surprised as to how light and free you feel. You find it so enjoyable to feel so loved and accepted.

As you approach the stairs, you feel vibrant and peaceful and alive. You feel pride about your achievements and all that you have overcome. You take a deep breath and start ascending the stairs. With step 10, you feel positive about your future. Step 9, you feel immense gratitude coursing through every fiber of your being, step 8, you feel so alive, step 7-you no longer feel the need to be a people pleaser, step 6- you affirm your freedom from addictive behaviors. Step 5- you feel so strong, step 4 your life is full of potential, step 3 you are awake, alert, and happy to be you, step 2, you are alert, your eyes start to flutter. Step 1- you become aware of your body and surroundings and fully restored to normal consciousness.

You are now free from addictions. Every time you feel the need to use substances or alcohol, or pornography, you will pinch yourself and affirm that your subconscious mind fully supports you. You will think and speak only positive thoughts about yourself. You are enough. You are loved, You are powerful. Om Shanti.

Guided Meditation for Sleep and Insomnia Relief (1 hour)

If you are having trouble falling asleep, then you have come to the right place. Try this meditation and simply relax and rift off to a restful sleep right away. All you have to do is get comfortable and relax. You can use headphones or earphones while listening to my voice.

Make sure that your bed is comfortable and switch off the lights if that is comfortable to you. There are no hard and fast rules here so simply do anything that relaxes you. You can choose to, if you wish, leave a small night light on. Just know that you are very safe and can choose to, if needed, come out of this meditation should the situation so demand.

But right now, the main aim is to get you to sleep deeply and restfully so you can wake up nourished and rested to take on the new day. This is very good for your health and productivity as a good night's sleep enhances concentration and releases tension and stress. Good sleep is also important to boost metabolism, rejuvenate your cells, and enhance your immunity. So, sleeping well for 7-8 hours each night is a must for overall health and well-being.

But right now, all you need to do is relax. If you haven't already, please close down your eyes. Let all the thoughts cease as you simply listen to my voice. I want you to take your attention to your abdomen. Notice how your abdomen rises and falls with each breath. So breathe in deeply and slowly and notice your abdomen rise. Then breathe out slowly and notice how your abdomen falls.

We will do this three times. Breathe in....feel the stomach rise....breathe out...feel the stomach fall.

Again, deep breath in, observe stomach rising and expanding, and deep breath out slowly, watching in your mind's eye the tummy fall down. And one more time, breathe in....and breathe out.

Now all you have to do is relax and listen to the sound of my voice, It is completely okay if you drift off into a relaxing and deep sleep. Every time I say the words **right now,** you will drift into deeper state of relaxation.

I am going to slowly count from 1 to 10. With each number, you will relax into a deep state of relaxation and feel the tension leaving your body one step at a time.

We are going from 1, relax and feel the tension leave your body

2 – feel the tension loose and fade away from your shoulders

3- relax

Right now – relax a bit more we go on to

4 simply let it all go

5- leave the day behind

6 right now, simply relax

7- let all the tension go away from the neck, arms, shoulders, and back.

8 let go and relax back into your soft and comfortable bed

9 right now we are going to drift deeper, and deeper and deeper.

10- you are totally relaxed.

We will now use progressive relaxation to relax each body part. You need not do anything, simply listen to my voice. All I want you to do RIGHT Now is to sink back into that comfortable pillow and bed. Simply drift off into the deepest sleep so you can wake up refreshed and happy.

But, right now, simply focus on my voice. You can judge my voice or think about it-may be it is too soft or too loud or even a bit dull and boring. But you can judge the quality of my voice as long as you still retain that ultimate relaxed state. Because, right now, that is of utmost importance to me: that you totally relax.

We will now take the attention to the right foot. Right now, simply feel the right foot completely. Feel the toes, feel its heel and feel the arch of the foot. How does it feel if you totally let the right foot grow heavier and sink fully into the soft bed beneath you? Right now, can you relax the right foot so that you are totally comfortable and relaxed? Good!

We will now take the attention to the left foot. Right now, simply feel the left foot completely –internally and externally. Feel the toes, feel its heel and feel the arch of the foot. How does it feel if you totally let the left foot grow heavier and heavier and sink the left fully into the soft bed beneath you? Right now, can you relax the left foot completely, and let its entire weight go into the surface underneath it so that you are totally comfortable and relaxed? Good!

Move your attention to the right leg just above the ankle. Scan the right leg completely from the right knee to the right ankle. Right now, can you relax this part completely? Simply let it go deeper into the bed underneath you. You can feel relaxation wash over the entire right leg from the knee to the ankle. Sink it deeper and deeper into the bed and let the leg's entire weight go into the bed. You are totally relaxed.

Now, move your attention to the left leg just above the left ankle. Scan the left leg completely from the left knee to the left ankle. Right now, can you relax this part of your body completely? Simply let the left leg go deeper into the bed underneath you. You can feel relaxation wash over the entire left leg from the knee to the left ankle. Sink it deeper and deeper into the bed and let the leg's entire weight go into the bed. You are so relaxed, so relaxed.

Right now, I want you to move upwards from the right knee to the top of the right thigh. You are going deeper into relaxation by scanning this area for any tension. If needed, right now, simply contract the muscles in this region for a few seconds and then let go. You are drifting deeper and deeper into total relaxation as the right thigh complete relaxes. You are so light and relaxed, you are totally relaxed. Right now, if it is possible, let the right thigh relax even more. This way, you can get a bit more comfortable if it is possible!

Right now, I want you to move upwards from the left knee to the top of the left thigh. You are going deeper into relaxation by scanning this area for any tension. If needed, right now, simply contract the muscles in this left thigh area for a few seconds and then let go. You are drifting deeper and deeper into total relaxation as your left thigh complete relaxes. You are feeling so light and relaxed, so totally relaxed. Right now, if it is possible, let the left thigh relax even more, then do it right away. This way, you can get a bit more comfortable and relaxed it is possible. All the tension is leaving your body bit by bit, one muscle at a time.

Right now, I want you to take your attention to the pelvis. Can you sink this area completely into the bed for me? This way, you can get a bit more comfortable and relax fully and deeply. If needed adjust your hips and buttocks so your pelvis naturally falls into a deeper relaxed state and comfortable state. Right now, if needed, contract your buttocks a bit for a few seconds and then let go. You are so relaxed, so relaxed. And you just hear my voice, nothing but my voice. Let your pelvic area relax, let it loose as you simply relax right now and only listen to my voice. You are so calm, comfortable, and so relaxed.

Right now, as you relax and let go of some more tension, I want you to take your attention to the stomach. You are going to sink the stomach and let it relax completely into the bed. If there is any tension in this region, you are going to command it away, right now. As you listen to my voice, simply become aware of the abdomen gently rising and falling as the stomach contracts and relaxes. Let my soothing voice simply guide you into the deepest state of relaxation. Feel all the organs inside the abdominal area relax and loosen completely.

In this ultra relaxed and comfortable state, I want you to move to the chest region where your heart center is located. Right now, simply feel the peaceful and gentle vibration emanating in your heart center. If you want, simply notice the breath filling the lungs and leaving the lungs. Relax completely right now for this is the time to totally let go and focus on loving yourself a little more. Relax and let go as you feel the chest rise and fall with every incoming and outgoing breath. Relax and feel unconditional love in the heart center. We are totally relaxed as love fills the heart and relaxation washes throughout the chest, lungs, heart and other organs. You feel total peace and all thoughts of the day fade away as you drift into a relaxing, peaceful, calming, and happy sleep.

Right now, we will scan the back. The back and shoulders accumulate a lot of tension and stress but we are going to let go of those and simply relax deeper and deeper. Right now, if needed you can roll or squeeze your shoulders but that is not compulsory if you don't want to. Simply loosen the tension from the muscles and let it all fade away as you drift into a relaxing sleep. Scan the shoulders, the upper back, and lower back and if you find any tension, simply dissolve it y relaxing more and more. If it helps, you can sink the entire weight of your back and shoulders into the bed or surface underneath you so that you can get a little more comfortable.

Right now, we will scan the neck. We want to relax the neck more and more so, if needed, let it sink into relaxation. If needed shift the position you are lying on so your neck can get even more relaxed. But this is not an absolute must and you can stay where you are if you are comfortable. All I want for you, right now, is to relax the neck as much as you can. Feel the tension leaving every cell as your neck completely relaxes into a deep, deep state of absolute relaxation. If needed, adjust your neck and body in such a way that you further deepen this state of relaxation. Right now, let go every tension from the neck, let go any though, an anxiety that may have accumulated stress in the neck.. For now it is time to relax and let all worries go away. This is your time to heal and relax and give some tender loving care to your body. You must take time daily for yourself no matter how busy you are. Right now, loosen every tendon, every nerve and sink deeper deeper and deeper into the most relaxed state.

Next, we will scan the face internally as well as externally. We will go deeper into relaxation as relax the forehead, the cheeks, the eye muscles and the mouth. Relaxation flows through the nose and lips, your mouth, your tongue, your teeth, and lips. You relax your clenched jaw and let go of any anger, negativity, or tension you may have unknowingly accumulated there. Right now, simply deepen the state of relaxation and let go of all the stress. This is anti-aging for your face as you let go of the tension that causes wrinkles and fine lines. Right now, take all the time you need because you deserve this time and you deserve this sleep. In your sleep, you heal and when you heal physically, emotionally, and even spiritually, you will find many positive changes occurring in many other aspects of your life as well.

We will, right now, move to the top of the head. We will totally relax and let go of any stress in the scalp, head, and back of the head. We will allow total relaxation, right now, to flow throughout the body.

You are now totally relaxed from head to toe. If needed, scan the body completely once again and remove any remaining tension there may be. This way, you can sink further into a relaxed state and completely become one with the universal laws. Now, you are in total harmony with the Laws of Vibration which decrees that anything you hold in your mind can be transferred and manifested into material world. That is the Law of attraction and we will use it now to get a deep, wonderful, and relaxing sleep. Because, in sleep you heal and in sleep you dream and dreaming is very good for you to manifest love, health, wealth, and peace. So, drift deeper into sleep and dream happy dreams which will come true as you get the ideas and strategies needed for manifesting them in reality.

You have taken this step for relaxation and that is indeed a great thing to do. Relaxing can help you sleep well and rest well. Right now, simply rest and drift off into dreamland. You can also use this deepened state of relaxation to shift from distractions and worries to peace and serenity. Your mind is very powerful and it can help you relax or it can let you worry all night. Right now, today, we will choose peace and serenity over worrying.

If you are awake and you find some traumatic thoughts still bothering you; it is okay. Simply accept the thought and resolve that you will continue to try and relax. You can, choose to either become aware of your breathing or, alternatively, choose to become aware of experiences outside you. You can, for example, become aware of the temperature in the room. Perhaps there are sounds or noises outside your house. These, in the past, may have been cues for you to get irritated or annoyed; but today, we will use them to relax and further the relaxation. Today, we will accept these distractions and simply choose to relax further and further.

Understand that you can choose to create peace and tranquility no matter where you are or what situation you may be undergoing. You must know that within your mind, there is a place where you can escape to for attaining this peace and serenity. Until hearing this, you were unaware of this place; however, now you know of it and you can choose to go there whenever you are faced with anxiety, insomnia, worries, or even trauma.

From this vantage you can create the life you want. You can drift, dream, or simply float in this new awareness. Using this creative part of your mind, you envision yourself in a beautiful place. Perhaps it is a place you have been before or entirely a new one. There is a clear blue sky and you are walking underneath this sky. You see a single blue cloud floating across the sky slowly and lazily.

You can see the edge of the cloud and It has a silver lining. There is pure divine and radiant energy that you feel in emanating from this cloud. You suddenly feel peace wash over you and you know that everything is going to be fine henceforth.

You now become even more aware of your mind's ability to let go of issues and problems. As the cloud drifts away into the distance, you feel your worries slip away as well. As the cloud disappears, your worries and anxieties disappear as well. At this point, right now, you also become aware of a deep sense of relaxation. You feel twice the sense of relaxation in the body and mind. You go down deeper into relaxed state and experience a sense of security. You feel you are taken care of. All your needs are addressed. All your desires are fulfilled. You feel loved. You feel calm. You feel unconditional love. You even feel grateful for the experiences you have had-good or bad experiences. These may be troubling you but you know that whatever has happened, will happens or is happening is always for your highest good. The divine takes care of you. With this knowledge you drift off into a peaceful sleep.

I am going to give you some suggestions now. You can choose to listen to them with your conscious mind or simply choose to drift, dream, and float. Worry not: your subconscious mind is listening to these suggestions no matter what you choose.

Understand that these suggestions are designed to help you sleep better. You asked me to make these suggestions to you when you came to this meditation to help you sleep better. So, it will be easier for you to internalize and experience these suggestions now or anytime you need a night of rest and tranquility.

Each night, you can choose to play this meditation. In fact; you are developing a strong desire to listen to this frequently. You will find that you can slip into a relaxed state within a millisecond the moment you hit the bed. You realize that the Universe wants your Highest Good. And with this awareness, you will find it easier and easier to relax within a short period of time

Because: when you know you are taken care of, you will relax completely. You will understand that there is a place inside of you where you can escape to for deepest relaxation, peace, and harmony. You will be able to immediately move your thoughts from external ones to peaceful and serene thoughts. You will find that part of mind where creativity and awareness are created. You will effortlessly slip inside that part and totally relax.

And as you relax, you will freely and lazily double the sense of relaxation and peace. You will feel a loosening of all the muscles which will double, even triple the relaxation. And all the while, you would know that you can easily slip out of this trance should the situation so demand. You can easily come out of the trance if needed and attend to any emergency.

But, right now, the time is to relax. And you double the sense of relaxation by becoming aware of your breathing. You also become aware, perhaps, of the sounds and noises around you. And as discussed, you use these to deepen your sense of relaxation by simply becoming aware of them and not attaching to them.

You will immediately move from external thoughts and noises into internal peace. You will automatically double, even triple the sense of relaxation by loosening the tension from the muscles.

This feeling of loosening the muscles can deepen the relaxed state more and more. You know that you can open your eyes at this point or choose to continue resting. It is entire up to you. You are feeling so good, so peaceful and so utterly relaxed that you choose to deepen the state of relaxation more and more.

There are no outside concerns here. You are so relaxed. You can continue enjoying this relaxed, peaceful state even while you are awake. And yes, you can even wake up at any point should the situation demand so. But right now, give yourself permission to deepen the relaxation. Simple loosen up every fiber of your being and sink into that warm and comfortable bed. And when you awake, you will feel so peaceful and refreshed.

However, the time to wake up is not now. For now, you will sleep and totally relax. You will continue to shift your awareness to that peaceful and serene state right inside you. Right now, you will choose to sleep. You will drift deeper and deeper into a relaxed, calming, and refreshing sleep.

I will now count backwards from 10 to 1. With each number, you will continue relaxing more and more. You will enjoy the sensation of heaviness and of coolness or warmth in your body. You will feel the warm bed, and you will relax

10..rest

9-perfect

8 relax more and more

7 slowly calmly drifting into a peaceful sleep

6 –you don't know where sleep begins

5- just experience the process

4- falling and falling into total relaxation

3-total peace total comfort

2- very good relax now-drifting to a point where awareness of awareness simply drifts off into the distance…

1-sleep…

Chapter 10 Guided Meditation for Releasing Anger (1 Hour)

Meditation is a great tool for releasing anger and letting go of past hurt. Anger is bad for you because it only hurts you and no one else. But I am so glad that you are here today.. The very fact that you have decided to meditate to release anger means that you wish to take back control of your life. You have come to realize and understand that only you suffer from anger. And anger is also probably getting in the path of all the things you want.

Anger helps when it is expressed positively. When it is channelize into hard work, the outcome can be positive. But, for that, you need to become aware of the negative emotions. Only then can you bring your mind into positivity and bliss.

It is important that you do this meditation at least once a day for 21 days. When you do so, your brain will be automatically rewired to release anger and you will become more relaxed and happier. You will learn to manage negative feelings better and also stay in the present moment.

It is best to do this meditation in the morning, although you can choose a time most convenient to you. It is best of you can avoid having a large meal prior to meditating.

As you get involved in this meditation, your day will go by better and you will find yourself relaxing even if there is a negative situation that triggers a negative feeling like anger or hurt. So please resolve to do this meditation for at least 21 days.

Before we begin, I would like you to get up and jog in place; just to get your blood warmed up. You can choose to march in your place or simply perform a few body rotations– rotating the neck, the wrists, the shoulders and the feet in clockwise and counterclockwise directions. A low-intensity workout is always great to get your mind focused and get those endorphins flowing; releasing negative emotions.

Okay-now that is done, we can start with our meditation.

Take a moment to find a comfortable spot where you won't be disturbed. Make sure to keep your gadgets and devices away for this hour. This is the time you need for getting your life back in control. So dedicate this daily hour to yourself and understand that you totally deserve this time.

Let us start by relaxing the body completely. Close your eyes, rest your palms in the lap, open towards the sky.

It is recommended that you sit down in a chair or on a yoga mat for this meditation. Do keep your spine erect. Let your body be relaxed and loose.

Become aware of your breath. Do not try to force your breath to change in any way. Simply become aware of it. Pay total attention to your breath. The incoming breath energizes the body, while the outgoing breath relaxes the body. So relax more and more with each outgoing breath.

We will now scan the body to relax each body part. Become aware of the top of your head. Is there any sensation that you notice there? Simply accept the sensation and breathe into it. Relax more and more as your awareness scans the entire scalp region. If there is any itching, irritation, or tingling, simply let it be. Let go of trying to control or change the sensations and simply accept it.

If any emotion like anger or hurt arises, simply understand that this is fleeting and that your mind has the power to ignore this feeling. So go ahead and ignore it completely and go back to scanning the head.

Move your awareness to the forehead. Let the forehead relax completely. Inhale and exhale…slowly, and fully.

One more deep breath in…hold the breath…and breathe out.

Take your awareness to the eye muscles. Relax the eyelids and the eyes and breathe in and out fully as you let go of any strain on the eyes.

Let the muscles of your cheek relax. Again, if you feel anger or upset, know that you have the power to let go. Simply relax more and more. Breathe in slowly and as you slowly, slowly breathe out, relax further and further.

Take the awareness to your jaw. Loosen up the jaw. Let your tongue roll forward and rest inside the lower part of the mouth. Relax your mouth and lips. One more deep breath in…hold the breath…and breathe out.

Let the breath become more and more steady and calm. When you are angry, notice how the breath becomes shorter. And as you breathe in an incomplete manner, your body gets limited oxygen which deprives all your cells of important nutrients. So, change your breath and you will change your life! Breathe in deeper and slower and see how all your problems, anger, tensions, and stress disappears.

So let us move on to the neck region. The neck and shoulders accumulate so much stress in them and that is why people complain of neck aches and back aches. So let us take a moment to focus on the neck. Is the neck hurting now? Maybe you feel an urge to move the neck and rotate it a bit. But we will resolve to sit still for this meditation and simply play the role of an observer.

So, simply become aware of the pain in your neck. One more deep breath in...hold the breath...and breathe out. Relax the neck completely with the outgoing breath.

Off we take our attention to the chest and the heart center. This is the location of the heart chakra – the seat of love. Any anger accumulated in the mind can impact the heart chakra. And that is why people can suffer heart attacks when the heart is filled with anger and hurt and hatred.

So, for a moment, focus on the heart center and think of love. You can even imagine the face of a person who is dearest to you. Fill your heart with immense love for this person. It can be someone close to you or even someone that you have romantic feelings for. It could be someone you consider a teacher or guru. Even if you are angry at the moment, we will only think of love, kindness and compassion for this person.

One more deep breath in...hold the breath...and breathe out. With the outgoing breath, relax more and more.

Drift downwards to the abdomen. Is there an unpleasant sensation in the abdomen? Perhaps anger is making your abdomen rise and fall rapidly. Remember, shorter breaths mean oxygen deprivation. So take a deeper fuller breath and feel the abdomen rise and fall.

With each outgoing breath relax the abdomen as well as your entire body. You can scan the stomach and other organs to find out where the anger is stored. Perhaps it is in your intestines or even in the stomach muscles which get contracted when we are angry. So let the muscles relax more and more and allow peace and joy to replace those negative feelings with.

One more deep breath in…hold the breath…and breathe out. And as you breathe out, let the body sink into a total relaxation.

Take the attention to the back. Scan the upper back and the lower back and relax all of the back muscles. We accumulate so much stress in this region. So simply observe any sensation of stress or pain and let it all go. One more deep breath in…hold the breath…and breathe out. With the outgoing breath, relax more and more. Relax the entire upper body.

Now we will move our attention to the lower body..starting with the hips. Relax the hips, the genitals, relax the pelvis. Breathe in deeply and fully and let it all out. We want all the tension to leave from the hips and buttocks. If needed, you can contract the hips and then relax totally. One more deep breath in…hold the breath…and breathe out. Relax more and more with each outgoing breath.

Your body is become totally relaxed and you just hear my voice…you hear nothing but my voice. We will now move our attention to the legs. Relax the legs starting with the thighs. Scan the thighs fully and remove any tensions there is by putting the entire weight of the thighs on the surface you are sitting on. One more deep breath in...hold the breath...and breathe out. With exhalation we will let out all the stress from the upper part of the legs before moving the attention to the lower part of the legs.

One more deep breath in...hold the breath...and breathe out.

Move your attention to the lower legs. Mentally scan the lower part of the legs and let out all the tension from them. Let the legs become heavier and relax totally on the surface you are sitting on. If needed, contract the calf muscles and then let the tension out by totally relaxing them.

One more deep breath in...hold the breath...and breathe out. With the out going breath, relax the lower part of your body totally.

Now move your attention to the feet. Relax the feet fully and let totally relaxation move from the heels to the toes. One more deep breath in...hold the breath...and breathe out.

If possible relax even deeper and deeper. Now you are totally relaxed. You are in perfect harmony with the universe.

I want you to think of a memory. A pleasant memory when you were totally happy. Happiest memory. It could be a memory from your childhood or your adulthood. It can be the day you got married, or the day you graduated or when you fell in love and they said yes. It could be the day your child was born. Any memory where you experienced total bliss.

I want you to summon those same feelings you felt on that day: happy, joyful, peaceful, blessed, blessed, confident, relaxed, energetic etc.

Summon those feelings and experience that same memory all over. We are going to relate these feelings to a word 'GREEN'. So you will associate the word GREEN to these beautiful feelings.

Every time I say the word GREEN, I want you to again experience the blissful, relaxed, confident, and blessed feeling. I want you to again live that joy.

Again when I say GREEN, summon those positive feelings in your heart, mind, and spirit.

Now, the next time you feel anger or other negative emotions, I want you to say the word GREEN. GREEN GREEN GREEN. You got it now. You will think of GREEN and immediately summon those positive feelings. You will totally forget anger, hurt, betrayal, and think only happy and positive thoughts.

And you will talk, and behave in way that will make you feel proud about yourself. Everytime you will notice GREEN color, you will immediately bring your mind back to that memory. For the next few days, you will be very aware of GREEN in your life. It could be at the traffic light or simply the trees and greenery around you.

And every time you notice GREEN, you will feel bliss, joy, and total happiness. You will consciously encounter GREEN and strengthen your resolve to improve your goal of reaching peaceful and happy thoughts. You will even implement this in your communication with your friends, family, colleagues, and every other interaction you have.

As you are relaxing more and more in this meditation, you will learn to become aware of each and every thought, feeling, and even sounds to guide you deeper and deeper. You are becoming more and more receptive to the words I speak.

Your past is losing its hold over you and you are coming more and more into present moment awareness. You find that small things no longer bother or irk you. You are totally awakened and relaxed. You are letting go of all the angry feelings and becoming more and more relaxed. GREEN GREEN GREEN – each time you will think of GREEN and summon that blissful and happy state or memory. You will do this even while you are awake and you start to feel your jaw tense and abusive words to come out of your mouth. You will not let the angry words come out...instead you will immediately think of GREEN and relax. You will become totally calm and you will even smile. And when the person sees this transformation in you, they will relax as well.

You have totally stopped getting angry and you have totally learnt how to deal with anger. Your subconscious mind has heard these suggestions and your consciousness desires to improve on all levels. And each and every time, this process will become more and more automatic. Whether you are awake or asleep, you will always be joyful and happy and in the present moment.

Soon your jaw will relax and your breathing will become deeper and slower. These are the first areas to get impacted by anger-the breath becomes shallow and your jaw tenses Your mind gets ready to blurt out expletives and angry curse words. But not any more. Cause you will immediately think of GREEN and you will totally relax and become so positive and happy. You will summon positive words and you will smile, laugh, and surrender the situation to the Higher Power. Soon you will find that the situation will take a turn for the better and you will get desired outcome-in fact the outcome will be better than the one you expected.

You have done excellent work today. You can take rest and now and let the subconscious mind listen to my suggestions.

I am calm

I am always happy

I am always safe

I let go of anger and hurt

I choose peace

I choose relaxation

Every situation works out in my favor and in the favor of all involved

Everyone who comes in contact with me feels peaceful, happy, calm, and relaxed

Every situation works out in the highest good for all

I choose happiness

I choose peaceful resolution to conflicts

I choose mindfulness

I select bliss

I am grateful

I am amazing

I am enough

I am loved

I am desired

I always acquire safe and happy friendships and relationships

This new information is now re-programming the old patterns and negative beliefs. You have a purpose and that is why you have come to this world. You have been given all the tools you need to in order to fulfill that purpose. You are now a calm, relaxed, and happy person. You now attract people to you as they feel safe and happy with you.. Your presence calms people and they drop negative feelings and anger and look up to you for guidance. You make them feel abundance. You make them see abundance and they leave you feeling deeply grateful and safe. They love you and whoever comes in contact with you find you to be that giving, abundant friend.

You are a good person. You are intelligent. You are strong. There is no room for anger hurt and negativity in your life because there Is pure bliss, gratitude, and happiness. All the old things that were holding you back are leaving you. You are a new person who sees gratitude and bliss in all things around you. You see your blessings and you are so grateful, so grateful

You now have a better outlook towards life and you now walk with a better self esteem. You have tossed out old garbage from the subconscious mind and you now have new positive feelings and patterns. You will remember GREEN and see GREEN and then consciously summon that positive memory right away.

You do not need those old patterns and beliefs. You do not need those angry thoughts. All you are left with is positive thoughts and feelings. All that you have is this new information that you are enough, you are happy, and you choose peace, calm, and joy.

The word GREEN brings positive thoughts and memories. You are totally blessed out. You will use these sessions which have been filled with positive insights. These insights are bits of wisdom. And once you have this wisdom, you can never use it. This new information will stay with you now. You are going to see yourself in a new way – a calmer, happier, more confident person. You are good, you are intelligent, and you are a kind person.

You have everything you need to do all that you have ever wanted to do.

With this new knowledge, you can wake up and come back to present moment awareness. In a moment, I will count from one to five. At five, you will emerge out of this session feeling totally calm and relaxed.

One – you are having happy thoughts and you are slowly emerging out of this trance

Two – Over the next few days, you will see a lot of GREEN and each time you do, be it at the traffic light, or a leaf or a green tree, you will feel happier. You will summon that happy memory and totally relax. You will bring your mind in present moment awareness and breathe slowly and deeply. And you will have total awareness of being kind, confident, happy, and positive because your subconscious mind has been reprogrammed with new beliefs.

Three – You will also feel a strong desire to listen to this again. You will listen to this audio for at least 21 days and you will immediately relax. You will get that you can go into a totally relaxed state within a millisecond.

Four-feeling so refreshed you are slowly becoming aware of your mind, body, and spirit.

Five-Open your eyes, feeling absolutely great!

Chapter 11 – Guided Meditation to get Over a Breakup (1 hour)

It is the hardest thing in life – the end of a relationship. The pain is akin to physical pain. It hurts and it cuts like a knife. But there is hope. It will take time and it is not easy, but you can overcome this. You have come this far. You have lived for so long without this person so you can and will be happy again.

Always know that the Universe has your best intention at its heart. That is why; you can rest assured that everything that is happening is for your highest good. It may not seem that way right now, but you will get over this. Soon you will be happy again and you will love again.

Before we begin, I would like you to get up and jog in place; just to get your blood warmed up. You can choose to march in your place or simply perform a few body rotations– rotating the neck, the wrists, the shoulders and the feet in clockwise and counterclockwise directions. A low-intensity workout is always great to get your mind focused and get those endorphins flowing; releasing negative emotions.

Okay-now that is done, we can start with our meditation.

I am so glad that you have decided to use meditation to get over a breakup and heartache. Meditation indeed helps and it can lessen the pain to a great degree. If you haven't been sleeping well, then this meditation will help soothe your mind and even lead you to a gentle sleep.

Take this time for yourself. Now is the time to love and care for yourself even more. It is a good idea to even do the Self-Love meditation in this audio book. Before you sit for this meditation I recommend that you sit with a crystal or a stone in your hand. It can be any crystal or stone. This stone will play a significant role in your journey of healing.

You can do this meditation any time of the day. I particularly recommend it when you feel overwhelmed with depressive thoughts. Anytime you feel you are on the point of a breakdown, you can take this up. Just make sure you are in a quiet place where you won't be disturbed for the duration of this hour.

Now is the time to relax. Now is the time to let all the negative feelings and emotions drift away. Surrender to the Higher Power and know that you are loved. I hope you are already comfortably seated. Relax the body fully and consciously relax all of the muscles of your body. Close your eyes gently if you haven't already done so. Keep the stone or crystal in your hand.

Take a deep breath in, and breathe out. Incoming breath energizes the body and mind while the outgoing breath relaxes the body. Relax more and more with each outgoing breath. If any emotions, thoughts, or feelings arise, let them. Let it out. It is okay to cry. But please resolve to sit still during the duration of this meditation.

We will start by relaxing the entire body starting with the head. Take your attention to the top of the head and feel the scalp internally and externally. Do not force anything. Simply become aware of the scalp with its thousands of hairs. Perhaps there is a tingling sensation in the scalp – it could be in the crown of the head or even the backside of the head. Maybe you feel an itch, or tightness. Let it be. Simply become aware of it. Do not try to change it or force it.

Slowly move the attention to the forehead. Perhaps you feel some tension or tightness in this area. Can you take a deep long breath in and relax your forehead as you breathe out? That's right – just let it all out.

We will traverse down the face now. Relax the cheeks, the lips, the nose, the jaw. Pay special attention to the eyes. Relax the eye muscles, the nerves leading from the eyes to the brain. Deep breath in and breathe out…as you breathe out, relax the eyelids and the eye muscles more and more. Relax the entire face.

Move your attention to the neck. First, scan the back of the neck and then the front. Internally and externally touch upon the nerves, the muscles, and the skin of the neck. Relax each and every cell in the front and backside of the neck. Deep breath in and breathe out…as you breathe out, relax the neck and the neck muscles more and more. Relax the entire back and front parts of the neck. Breathe in and breathe out slowly and fully.

Take your awareness to the torso and the upper body. This is the part of your body that protects your heart, lungs and other vital organs. With your mind's eye, scan the back and front of the upper body and progressively relax them both. First, relax the shoulders, the chest, and the abdominal area. Then, relax the upper back, the spine, and the lower back. Breathe in deeply and slowly and breathe out. Let the torso just go limp. Relax all the internal organs in the body as well. With each outgoing breath relax more and more. Relax the arms, the front and back of the upper arm, the lower arm, your wrists, palms, and the fingers all the way down to the finger tips.

Take your attention to your lower body. Relax the lower body completely starting with the hips, the pelvis, the back of the thighs, the front of the thighs, both the knees, the upper part of your legs, the lower part of your legs all the way to your toes.

You are now totally relaxed. Breathe in slowly and fully. I want you to slowly expand your stomach when you inhale. Go ahead do it now- inhale and expand the stomach. And as you exhale, pull back the navel towards the spine.

Again inhale-bloating the tummy – and exhale drawing the belly to the spine.

We will do this one more time – inhale- expand the stomach fully..and exhale-puling in the stomach and bringing it towards the spine.

Now relax.

Relax more and more.

In your mind's eye, you see a door ahead of you in a distance. It is about 10 steps away from you. You need to take 10 steps towards the door and with each step you will let go of the sorrow and emptiness you may be experiencing.

You see, this door is the gateway to a new life and new possibilities. At the moment you may be feeling that your life is over without your ex. But beyond the door, there awaits a happier life, a life where you can be your cheerful self.

So take one step and feel the loneliness and anxiety fade away.

Take step 2 and you are letting it go.

Step 3- and you surrender fully to the Higher Power

Step 4 – You know you will feel alive, energetic, and enthusiastic again

Step 5 – A new and improved life awaits you as you step towards the door

Step 6 – You feel hope, joy, and cheer

Step 7 – You feel an excitement coursing through your veins

Step 8 – You feel more and more alive

Step 9 – Your heart is racing as you feel eager and curious to see what awaits you behind that door

Step 10 – As you near the door, a soft golden glow is emanating through the door.

You step through the door in the most beautiful garden you have ever seen in your life. As far as your eyes can see, there is greenery and flowers in every color awaiting you. The garden has lush green grass and there is a pathway with stones for you to walk on. On each side of this pathway, there are millions of flowering shrubs lining the sides of the pathway.

The air is heavily perfumed with the sweet smelling flowers. As you step in the pathway, you feel all of the remaining tension and sorrow leaving your body and mind. You feel comfortable and relaxed and, most importantly, hopeful. You feel a strange kind of joy bubbling within you.

As you walk down the path, you feel the pleasant and gentle breeze caressing your body. You also feel the warm sun comfortable on your back and neck. The temperature is just right – not hot, not cold, perfect. You walk on through the garden and arrive at a beautiful pond. You dip your toes into the water and find that it has the perfect temperature.

You sit on a nearby rock and keep dipping your toes in the water. The gentle breeze soothes your body and mind. You feel you have arrived home. This is a place that you know you can be yourself and rest and relax totally.

You feel something akin to gratitude and warmth in this place. The sunlight bathes your body and relaxes and rejuvenates every cell. You sit on a comfortable rock still dipping your feet in the water. The cool water soothes your tired feet and legs. The warm sunlight bathes you in loving energy.

At this point you are totally relaxed in this loving environment. Your body is so relaxed and you wonder if you can relax some more. Suddenly you see a beautiful stone in the soil at your feet. You pick it up and rinse it in the water. The stone feels cool and comfortable and suddenly you feel a peaceful and loving sensation in your body.

You are transformed to a time when you felt totally loved and joyful. The stone leaves a wonderful feeling in your heart. You feel confident and blessed. You suddenly are reminded of all things that are going on well in your life.

You feel blessed for the abundance surrounding you.

The stone is a powerful reminder that you are enough. That you are loved. That you are powerful. That you love yourself and are very happy with your self.

As you continue holding the stone, loving energy radiates from it throughout your being. Every cell is now rejuvenated and you feel totally alive and vibrant and joyful. You feel blissful energy coursing through every cell of your body.

Taking a deep breath in you soak in this loving sensation. And as you exhale you savor the love and warmth emanating from the stone.

I will now take you through some affirmations. Affirmations help reinforce new patterns on the subconscious mind. You can continue relaxing and simply hear my voice..

I am loved

I am enough

I am amazing

I am confident

I am healthy

I am beautiful

I am energetic

I am enthusiastic

I am awesome

I am balanced

I am God's highest creation

I am an important part of this universe

I have a purpose

I am releasing the past

I am always joyful

I forgive myself

I forgive my ex

I have power over my life

I trust myself

I trust the Higher Power

Only the best happens to me

There is something better waiting for me

I am already whole and complete

I am a love magnet

I am love

I see love everywhere I go

I am enough

I matter

I have a lot to offer

I am kind and loving

I learn new things everyday

I am constantly improving and bettering myself

I honor the love I share

I am joyful in any given situation

I am likeable, loveable, and attractive

I am allowing myself to feel love again

I am allowing myself to feel happy again

My heart is open to love

I give love and share love easily

Everyday I am healing

Every day I am getting better and better

I am capable of trusting myself again

I am worthy

I am worthy of love

I am in abundance

Abundance and love surround me

I see abundance in every aspect of my life

My relationships are very safe

I only attract those relationships that are good for me

I only attract trustworthy, honest, and loving relationships

My body is strong and healthy

I take the time to workout and eat healthy

I nourish my body and mind

I am beautiful inside and out

I am willing to forgive myself and others

I love myself fully

I have the power to transform my pain into wisdom

I choose love

I am reclaiming my heart

I am reclaiming my mind

I am reclaiming my time

I am reclaiming my life

I am reclaiming my kindest, most generous, and most useful power

I am free

I am whole

I am here for a reason

I am allowing my pain to help me do better

I am finding comfort in my family and friends

I am committed to taking care of myself

I am healing
Each day, I am getting healthy and happy

Today I am pressing the restart button

I am a miracle

I am assertive

I am attentive

I am attractive

I am authentic

I am blessed

I am brilliant

I am caring

I am compassionate

I am complete

I am confident

I am courageous

I am worthy and there is nothing on this earth that can keep me from my good or take away my worth

I am strong

I get the help when I need

Everyone around me loves me

I am self-aware

I am superior to negative thoughts and low actions

I acknowledge my own self-worth

I am a powerhouse

I am indestructible

I am whole and complete

I am loved

I am loved by God

I am loved by the Universe

I am healing

I allow myself to fully feel what I am experiencing

I choose me

I release all tension from my body and mind

I relax fully

My situation simply is – it isn't good or bad –it simply is

I am in control of my stress levels

I am enough

I am enough

I am enough.

With these affirmations, you feel recharged. You are totally in control of yourself. You feel powerful. And the stone you hold in your hand is the reminder of good things to come. You hold the stone in your hand and take it near your heart. The stone glows and radiates warmth. And you feel unconditional love and joy wash over you. You feel everything will be alright. You know it-you say it-you feel it. You just know that all is going to work well in your favor. And the best part is that you can come to this empowering feeling anytime you wish. Each time you feel low or depressed, you can hold the stone in your hand and take it near your heart center and immediately relax. You will immediately go into a totally relaxed state. You will understand you are enough and you will do just what it takes to get through this phase. You will, right away, go into a blissful state and you will experience immense joy and you will feel confident, loved, and happy.

With these new patterns of learning, you walk back the way you cam. You pass the beautiful garden back through the perfumed air and the warm sunlight. You see the door in the distance and you realize that beyond the door there is hope and new beginning. You feel alive and you feel unconditional love for yourself.

I will count down from 10 to 1. Each number brings you closer and closer to the door. With each number, you will fill every cell of your body with deep unconditional love, hope, and energy.

Step 10...you are releasing any remaining negativity

9- you feel so alive –there's a consciousness of abundance in your consciousness which is phenomenal- it is not just out there for someone else..it is yours

8 – you feel vibrant and alive there is an unexplained self love and unconditional universal love seeping through every cell of your being.

7- you take a step close to your new life where beautiful new beginnings await you

6 – you feel excitement and hope and joy stirring within the depths of your heart

5- one more step closer to love and belonging and acceptance

4- more beautiful consciousness in every cell of your body

3- opening the door you become aware of your body and surroundings

2- you are loved –you are loved – you are loved!

1-Eyes open!

You are so happy and joyful and loving. Love emanates from your being attracting loving energy towards you. Now go out there and share the love and spread the love. Om shanti-shanti-shanti!

www.ingramcontent.com/pod-product-compliance
Lightning Source LLC
Chambersburg PA
CBHW070909080526
44589CB00013B/1233